POWER
STRATEGIES OF
JESUS CHRIST

POWER
STRATEGIES OF
JESUS CHRIST

PRINCIPLES OF LEADERSHIP
FROM THE GREATEST MOTIVATOR OF ALL TIME

HARRY A. OLSON

GRAMERCY BOOKS
NEW YORK

Scripture quotations are taken from the Revised Standard Version,
copyright © 1946, 1952, 1971 by the Division of Christian Education
of the National Council of Churches of Christ in the USA and used
by permission.

This 1999 edition is published by Gramercy Books,™
an imprint of Random House Value Publishing, Inc.,
201 East 50th Street, New York, New York 10022,
by arrangement with Liguori Publications/Triumph Books.

Gramercy Books™ and colophon are trademarks of
Random House Value Publishing, Inc.

Random House
New York • Toronto • London • Sydney • Auckland
http://www.randomhouse.com/

Printed and bound in the United States of America

Library of Congress Cataloging–in–Publication Data

Olson, Harry A., 1944-
    Power strategies of Jesus Christ : principles of leadership from
the greatest motivator of all time / Harry A. Olson.
        p.   cm.
    Originally published: Tarrytown, N.Y. : Triumph Books, c1991.
    Includes bibliographical references.
    ISBN 0-517-20334-0
    1. Leadership—Psychological aspects. 2. Leadership—
Religious aspects—Christianity.   I. Title.
    [BF637.L4047   1999]
    158'.4—dc21   98-47544
                                                                     CIP

                        8 7 6 5 4 3 2 1

To the glory of God
and in loving memory of
Lillie Tekla Charlotte Olson,
my aunt,
who, after my parents,
had the greatest impact on
my spiritual development

ACKNOWLEDGMENT

I wish to thank my wife, Carol, for her loving support and many hours of typing and proofing this manuscript, and my son, Dave, who shared me with this project. Thanks also to Jeff Herman and Deborah Adams, my agents, who believed in this project and were so helpful in the proposal stage and in making this book a reality. Also, I deeply appreciate the support from the Reverend Kevin Gillory, the Reverend Lee Mebust, Alan Schneider, and other friends too numerous to mention here who took an active interest in this book and who encouraged me onward.

Harry A. Olson

CONTENTS

Contents

INTRODUCTION

Business has lost its sanity.

The insider trading scandal, hostile takeovers and acquisitions by the score, the "business is war" mentality with the deification of Attila the Hun and Sun Tsu, sacrificing long-term gains on the altar of the fast buck, cutthroat competition.

These and other recent factors have eroded public confidence in our businesses, reduced employees' loyalty to their companies, and cost us our competitive edge in the global marketplace. With all our technological advances, when it comes to respect for human life and welfare in corporations, we are still in the dark ages. Stress and burnout are at an all-time high. What's more, we're now seeing a whole new set of mental health problems—reasonably emotionally healthy people experiencing conflict in having to adapt to organizations that are patently sick!

People are recognizing that the yuppie dream of American success is shallow and unsubstantial. The thirty-something generation is finding what many have known all along—money does not buy happiness. More and more in my counseling and consulting practice, I see burnt-out twenty-eight-year-olds struggling with disillusionment in their careers. All across our great nation, people are crying out for meaning in their daily work activities, yet few business leaders appear to understand.

The human cost of doing business has never been greater. Just look around. Ethical and moral compromises are a matter of course in one's climb to the top. After all, "business is war," and there will be casualties. Yet while so many business leaders are playing soldier, glorying in the war games, they fail to recognize that the military model itself is doomed to ultimate defeat. Glowing mission statements, competitor intelligence, and fancy game plans and market share mean little when the rank and file feel underutilized, unfairly treated, and unloved, and customers feel poorly served.

Sun Tsu and Attila the Hun don't cut it. There needs to be a new model of business leadership. A model founded on peace, not war; on unity, not division; on caring, not greed. A model that supports and enhances the potential greatness and beauty that also exists in American business. A model that values body, mind, and spirit as the vital necessities of enterprise. A model that values significance versus superiority.

Paradoxically, this new model has always been with us. He's just been waiting behind the scenes to be recognized and utilized. This model is Jesus Christ and he is probably saying today about business what he said on that first Palm Sunday long ago as he wept over Jerusalem, "Would that even today you knew the things that make for peace! But now they are hid from your eyes" (Luke 19:42).

Who was Jesus? Mankind has been divided—often bitterly—over this issue for two millennia. His followers echo the confession of St. Peter, "Thou are the Christ, the son of the living God"; for many others, this is a stumbling block. Most agree, however, that Jesus of Nazareth, the lowly carpenter's son, grew into a charismatic leader of the first order. He was an itinerant preacher, great prophet, and probably the greatest psychologist and motivator of his day.

Yet he was also the Son of God. Doesn't it stand to reason,

then, that he exemplified absolutely the best, most knowledgeable techniques in motivating and managing people? Furthermore, his little band of followers were all volunteers. He offered
no salary, no perks, none of the corporate contracts that tie
employees to the organization. Yet what he offered was so powerful that his disciples—the original twelve and countless others down through the ages—set themselves against family,
friends, principalities, and powers for his sake, and followed
him relentlessly, even to the death.

What did Jesus offer? From the Christian perspective, the
answer is simple. Salvation: new life here on earth and a guaranteed place in the Kingdom of God for eternity. No one else
can offer that. So let's put faith aside for a moment and look at
the sociocultural side of the Jesus phenomenon, the secular
perspective. Let's look at Jesus the leader, Jesus the manager. At
a strictly human level, at which we operate, what can this man
who convinced so many that he was the Messiah teach us today
about leadership, about management, about motivation?

Everything—at least everything that really counts. His is the
Greatest Story Ever Told. Jesus was the turning point of human
history. The world has never been, nor could it be, the same
ever again. How did one poor, lone Galilean preacher turn the
world upside down? Today's leaders and managers would
profit well from learning how he did it.

We know that the Word of God made Christianity take hold.
God's Spirit moved in the hearts of people, leading them to
faith. Yet Jesus lived and ministered on earth as a man. He
related to people in human terms, in ways that they could
understand. Jesus not only performed miracles; he also used
extremely powerful but strictly human techniques to draw people to himself.

This book, then, is a tactical manual for transformational
leadership. Its purpose is to analyze and clarify in a simple,
direct way the subtle people-moving methods of the Master so
that today's leaders can emulate them. Therefore, this book
does not deal with the Resurrection, nor with Jesus' miracles,

because, while we can learn much from them, we cannot replicate those. Rather, our spotlight shines on Jesus the man, the leader, the motivator, the model. By examining his everyday actions as they are portrayed in the Gospels, we discover enlightened ways to accomplish healthy goals in business and in life.

Can we work modern miracles? Yes, indeed! The age of miracles isn't gone, it's only just begun! St. Paul stated, "I can do all things through Christ who strengthens me" (Phil. 4:13). God's promises and power are at our disposal today. Just as they were to Jesus' disciples and other followers down through the ages. By modeling the Master in a spirit of prayer and openness to divine leading, we become the channel through which the Holy Spirit may move with power in the hearts and lives of those we touch as leaders. Turning water into wine is nothing compared with what God challenges and empowers us to do. God never takes a vacation. When we don't notice God's presence, it isn't because God is absent, but because we failed to pay attention. When we can't hear God's voice, it's because there's static in the channel—the static of our own reluctance, ego, or self-doubt.

A tactical manual is not meant to be a spiritual treatise. Nor are most of the tactics described spiritual in nature. They make perfect sense and are very powerful strictly from a human point of view. Yet when we apply the Master's tactics that follow, which he taught us through his actions, with the same spirit of love, concern, confidence, and openness to God's full power, miracles happen.

Business needs to be transformed. This is our challenge. God belongs not only at the center of the church altar but also at the head of the boardroom table. As a leader, therefore, you have a special mission. God will equip you for mighty acts. And when you take the lead, God is with you and never will desert you. And if God is for you, no one can prevail against you. You have His Word on it!

POWER
STRATEGIES OF
JESUS CHRIST

1
THE SPIRIT OF LEADERSHIP

Your primary task as a leader is to empower your followers. Only then can your team's full potential be maximized. As Lao Tsu put it, the hallmark of the inspired leader is that his or her followers could say, "We did it ourselves." Anything less is a distortion, and misses the mark.

In today's rapidly changing society—in our businesses, schools, churches, teams, organizations, and clubs—inspired leadership is critical. As competition and confusion increase, effective leadership is necessary to channel the change and activity in positive directions which not only meet the situational demands but also fulfill the multivarious needs of the persons involved.

Jesus Christ is the ultimate model of transformational leadership. He was a marvelous motivator, a superb tactical leader. But tactics, to be lastingly effective, must rest on a solid foundation. That bedrock is the person of the leader himself or herself: an inner spirit that commands and compels loyalty and action, not through autocratic means, which ultimately fail, but through inspiration in the heart and soul as well as the mind of the follower.

Jesus possessed such a spirit. So can you. Jesus has often been called "charismatic," and so he was, but this is a shallow compliment. One can be charismatic and still be phony and insincere. Charisma often is only skin-deep. Jesus' inner spirit, which empowered his leadership skill, goes much deeper. Even "noncharismatic" people who develop this inner spirit and practice the tactics in this book can become effective transformational leaders.

As we study Jesus' life and actions from a leadership perspective, we discover four traits that comprise the spirit of leadership. These are traits of his inner self that showed forth in his daily actions, that made him convincing and undergirded his power with people.

Fortunately, these traits can be developed and nurtured in each of us. Backed by the power of the Holy Spirit in our lives, they will enable us to achieve modern-day miracles as we ignite the spark of power, faith, and love in our followers. That is what transformational leadership is truly all about.

The first of these traits is *congruence*. Jesus was real, he was himself. Jesus preached, "Turn the other cheek," and at his arrest in the Garden of Gethsemane,

> . . . when those who were about him saw what would follow, they said, "Lord, shall we strike with the sword?" And one of them struck the slave of the high priest and cut off his right ear. But Jesus said, "No more of this!" And he touched his ear and healed him.
>
> Luke 22:49–51

He preached, "Love your enemies," and then, from the cross, prayed, "Father, forgive them for they know not what they do."

Jesus practiced what he preached. He expressed the full range of human emotion and was totally honest in his dealings with others. He wept over Jerusalem, and also drove the money changers out of the Temple. He healed the sick and vehemently confronted his opponents.

Jesus' honesty and sincerity ring out clearly from the Gospel accounts. He knew well the importance of his mission and his central role in human history, yet he was not arrogant, nor did he puff himself up or present an air of phony importance. In short, he was not on an ego trip. Jesus had a key role in God's plan; he presented himself humbly yet assertively. He was able to make himself and his role synonymous. In his own life, he was the prime example of what he taught to others.

Second, Jesus demonstrated *courage*.

> And Jesus entered the temple of God and drove out all who sold and bought in the temple, and he overturned the tables of the money-changers and the seats of those who sold pigeons. He said to them, "It is written, 'My house shall be called a house of prayer'; but you make it a den of robbers."
>
> Matt. 21:12, 13

In this one act, Jesus challenged a whole social, political, and religious institution which had been going on for many years. For that action alone, Jesus could have been crucified.

On numerous occasions, Jesus challenged the religious leaders of his day for their duplicity and hypocrisy. Perhaps his ultimate act of courage was his Palm Sunday entry into Jerusalem, knowing that there he would meet his death.

Courage is infectious. When the leader acts courageously, the followers also pump up their nerve. They will all take greater risks, and therefore accomplish greater deeds. Yet action needs something else to be effective. Blind acting out often causes more trouble than it is worth. Action needs direction, a target.

Jesus provided that direction. He had, thirdly, *commitment* to his mission and tremendous singleness of purpose. His courage was fueled by his commitment, and his message was consistent and clear. All of his actions and words always pointed in the same direction. In various ways, he was always driving home the same message—the Kingdom of God.

Jesus' mission fueled and directed his courage. When I was in college, I was planning on becoming a missionary. I was very impressed by the numerous missionaries I had met, and I read the biographies of several more. As I read and talked with these people, I discovered that these missionaries had six characteristics in common—six qualities that Jesus also must have possessed—that gave them the direction, drive, and staying power to thrive in the face of severe adversity:

- *Vision of human need and possibilities.* They have the ability to see something where there is now nothing. The mission is sparked with creativity and strong empathy.
- *Identification with a worthy cause.* They identify with something larger than themselves, which provides personal meaning.
- *Sense of one's own importance in promoting the cause.* This is not egotism, but a healthy respect for one's role, talents, and capabilities. The greatness of the cause promotes a healthy humility.
- *Indestructible courage and commitment.* Do or die. These people possess the ability to hang in there when the going gets tough.
- *Onward-outward orientation and drive.* They look for new avenues and opportunities of service. They have an expansionist orientation that is quite akin to that of many entrepreneurs.
- *Never-ending hope and faith.* This is the quality that provides the spark for mighty deeds.[1]

You may have noticed that the first letters of these six qualities spell VISION. No accident. Like Jesus, the missionary is a visionary.

Jesus was true to this mission to the very end, giving it "the last full measure of devotion"[2]:

> Then Jesus went with them to a place called Gethsemane,
> and he said to his disciples, "Sit here, while I go yonder
> and pray." And taking with him Peter and the two sons of
> Zebedee, he began to be sorrowful and troubled. Then he
> said to them, "My soul is very sorrowful, even to death;
> remain here, and watch with me." And going a little far-
> ther he fell on his face and prayed, "My Father, if it be
> possible, let this cup pass from me; nevertheless, not as I
> will, but as thou wilt."
>
> Matt 26:36–39

How far are you willing to follow your dream?

Jesus' sense of mission and clear direction were infectious.
Inspired through his congruence, courage, and apparent winning personality, people dropped what they were doing and
followed him instantly. Here was a man they could trust, whose
power and belief in himself and in them could get them through
the difficulties they would face. Here was their champion. Here
was their Messiah.

Once he earned their allegiance, how did he maintain it day
in, day out, in times of poverty and heavy political pressure?
The aforementioned traits motivated his followers significantly, but one more characteristic was necessary to seal their
loyalty and to keep them faithful even after Jesus was no longer
with them. Without this trait, Jesus' message would have been
hollow, and his following may have collapsed.

And fourth, Jesus had compassion. Consider the following
passages:

> And Jesus went about all the cities and villages, teaching
> in their synagogues and preaching the gospel of the king-
> dom, and healing every disease and every infirmity. When
> he saw the crowds, he had compassion for them, because
> they were harassed and helpless, like sheep without a
> shepherd.
>
> Matt. 9:35, 36

> Then Jesus called his disciples to him and said, "I have
> compassion on the crowd, because they have been with me

now three days, and have nothing to eat; and I am unwilling to send them away hungry, lest they faint on the way." And the disciples said to him, "Where are we to get bread enough in the desert to feed so great a crowd?" And Jesus said to them, "How many loaves have you?" They said, "Seven, and a few small fish." And commanding the crowd to sit down on the ground, he took the seven loaves and the fish, and having given thanks he broke them and gave them to the disciples, and the disciples gave them to the crowds. And they all ate and were satisfied; and they took up seven baskets full of the broken pieces left over. Those who ate were four thousand men, besides women and children.

Matt. 15:32–38

And a leper came to him beseeching him, and kneeling said to him, "If you will, you can make me clean." Moved with pity, he stretched out his hand and touched him, and said to him, "I will; be clean." And immediately the leprosy left him, and he was made clean.

Mark 1:40–42

Jesus was the soul of compassion, as these and numerous other instances in the Gospels prove. Love was the backbone of Jesus' ministry, and that love had to emanate if he was to be believed.

Today, it's popular for our business leaders to study military strategy as an analog to doing business. We're told that business is war. Yet let us never forget that while a general's dramatic deeds of derring-do will inspire loyalty, such deeds won't necessarily keep it. Some powerful generals were feared by their troops, but the greatest military leaders, such as George Washington, were loved by them.

How did Jesus demonstrate his love and the other traits that made him the inspirational leader that he was? This leads us to the main thrust of this book—the strategies themselves.

Many books on leadership focus on what the leader does. But, to reiterate what was said at the outset of this chapter, the methods have meaning and validity only in the context of what kind of person the leader is and what values and beliefs he or she demonstrates. Faith is personal. Followers don't believe in actions; they have faith in the *person* who carries out those actions.

Jesus as Strategist

When you think of Jesus, what comes to mind? A wandering preacher, a missionary, a healer, a magician, the Son of God? The Gospels portray Jesus as all of the above. The Gospels are, in fact, a hodgepodge of stories, sayings, and eyewitness accounts of Jesus' life and ministry. They do not read like a systematic chronology, but rather they present snatches, vignettes, incidents. In some ways, they seem disjointed.

When you read the Gospel accounts carefully, however, you can't help but be impressed by Jesus' finesse. More than being a charismatic preacher and miracle worker, Jesus had a superb grasp of timing, of drama, and of the human condition. He knew precisely what actions and words would make the greatest, most lasting impression on heart and soul. Therefore, he orchestrated many of his activities to achieve powerful impact. His baptism, his Palm Sunday entrance into Jerusalem, his casting the money changers out of the Temple—these were not spontaneous acts. They were undoubtedly planned and executed to create a specific impression, capitalizing on symbolism and often drama.

Of course, Jesus was also spontaneous, but behind the scenes, his mission was clear in his mind, and his strategy, based on that mission, was solidly and caringly carried out in his day-to-day activities, bringing consistency to word and deed.

Strategy, in the service of mission, carried out with compassion, all of which is true, honest, and congruent with the person of the leader himself or herself—this is the spirit of transformational leadership.

2
ASSUME YOUR AUTHORITY

And when he entered the temple, the chief priests and the elders of the people came up to him as he was teaching, and said, "By what authority are you doing these things, and who gave you this authority?" Jesus answered them, "I also will ask you a question; and if you tell me the answer, then I also will tell you by what authority I do these things. The baptism of John, whence was it? From heaven or from men?' And they argued with one another, "If we say, 'From heaven,' he will say to us, 'Why then did you not believe him?' But if we say, 'From men,' we are afraid of the multitude; for all hold that John was a prophet." So they answered Jesus, "We do not know." And he said to them, "Neither will I tell you by what authority I do these things."

Matt. 21:23–27

(*Parallel texts:* Mark 11:27–33; Luke 20:1–8)

What really went on in this interchange? The chief priests weren't curious. Nor did they care whether or not anyone gave Jesus permission to preach in the Temple. Their question was a challenge, a frontal attack: "What right do you have to teach or heal?" Jesus could have answered with an explanation, but, rather, he fired back with a riddle. This was a power play on the part of the priests. Jesus held his ground, refused to become defensive, and put the priests in their place.

His method? He simply returned their question with a question. Jesus often did this when he perceived that his opponents were insincere in their queries or were trying to trap him. A question in itself is a power tactic. It has an implicit demand quality about it: a question demands an answer, and assumes the questioner has a right to know that answer. In power terms, then, asking a question places the asker above the one being asked, who is expected to comply by answering.

For Jesus to have offered an explanation to the priests, whom Jesus perceived would not have listened anyway, would have been a power loss. Rather, he trumped them by posing a question in return (matching power for power), a "trick" question that he knew they couldn't answer. Since the priests could not answer it, Jesus actually outpowered them. He was one up.

Jesus' tactic cited here is but one example of a broad fundamental issue of leadership that Jesus demonstrated repeatedly. He never backed down, he never gave his opponents the advantage. He never went on the defensive when challenged. He always acted as if he had *every right* to do and say what he did. He came across looking and acting totally together and secure.

In short, he assumed his authority. The word *assume* means two things: (1) to take on the responsibility for, and (2) to accept without question, to believe implicitly and completely. When it came to his authority, Jesus did both.

Assume your authority as leader using both meanings of the word. Once authority is granted to you, it is yours. You needn't defend it repeatedly nor become insecure when challenged. Act out your authority with total assurance. You don't owe explanations, so don't give them. Do it, don't talk about it.

Assume your authority and act accordingly. So simple, so obvious. Why is this tactic even worth mentioning? Authority is at once a structural, social, political, symbolic, and psychological issue. In the structural sense, authority goes with a particular position on the organizational chart. Your formal position grants you certain rights and also provides certain constraints. Socially, authority requires other people. Authority means nothing in isolation. Rather it interfaces with other roles, and with the people who fill those roles. Politically, how much authority/power do you have, who supports you, who opposes you? Is the grantor of your authority strong or weak? Symbolically, your authority *means something* to others. How do they view you, your role, and your ability to fill your position? It is at the political and symbolic levels that you will be made or broken in your attempts to wield your authority.

Assuming authority is both an outward tactic and an inward attitude. Fundamentally, how others view you and your role, and whether they cooperate with you, depends in large measure on the psychological dimension—how *you* view your authority. If you assume your authority as Jesus did his—that is, take it for granted—in a healthy, positive, assertive way, you encourage others to see you as effective. They are more likely to accept your authority without question. If you approach your role with self-doubt, that insecurity will be transmitted to your followers and opponents, undermining their confidence in you. No one else will accept your authority more than you accept it yourself.

How you accept and adjust to your leadership role directly affects how you act that role out. This in turn determines how well others will let you pull it off. That's right: *let* you. You can't be a leader without followers. Likewise, powerful opponents can hamstring you so much that effective leadership becomes impossible, in spite of how much ascribed authority you have been granted. The truly powerful leader understands well the limits of his or her control.

Leadership, then, is a confidence game: your confidence in yourself and in your followers, your followers' confidence in you and in themselves, and your opponents' view of your power and formidability. Therefore, once you have been promoted or elected to a position of leadership, you must hit the ground running, as Jesus did, acting with a total display of self-confidence and solidity.

Assuming your authority is a key issue, because there are several psychological variables that make it easier said than done.

- *Authority and power are very different.* Authority is ascribed. It goes with the job title, regardless of who fills that position. It grants you certain *powers* and hold you accountable for certain responsibilities. But let's never confuse authority with *power*. Power is a personal factor. It comes from within. Authority gives you the shoes, while power determines in part how well you can fill them. "Assuming your authority" means "acting powerfully, in a positive way, with inner strength and confidence."

- *Authority can tempt you into an ego trip.* The desire for authority and for power over others is a very seductive goal. It's probably true that the higher one goes within an organization, the stronger one's "power drive" is and the more one actually grooves on being the boss. This is natural, normal, and possibly necessary in order not to burn out under the heavy responsibilities that accompany high-level authority. The danger lies in becoming overly impressed with one's own importance. The proper place and use of ego will be discussed in the next chapter.

- *Many leaders and successful people feel insecure.* According to psychologist Joan C. Harvey, approximately 70 percent of high-achieving people feel like fakes. The imposter phenomenon is a psychological pattern in which those who possess it feel that they don't deserve their success, that they are phonies who haven't really got what it takes to carry out the responsibilities that go with their success. These people are often driven to achieve, but worry that each new success will reveal that they are actually frauds. They don't believe that their achievement is real but that rather, deep down, they are incompetent.[1]

A recent study by Gerald Ferris, Ph.D., a management professor at Texas A & M, showed that brownnosing really does impress the boss. Flatterers, he found, get better performance evaluations. Why? Because many bosses are insecure or have big egos.[2] Feelings of personal insecurity make you more vulnerable to manipulation by others.

Yet insecurity feelings are real, and if we're honest with ourselves, we have all felt that way at one time or another. Insecurity tends to mount more quickly the faster we rise within an organization, or the greater the jump from where we were last to our new level of authority.

The worst thing you can do about your insecurity feelings is not to admit them to yourself. They are very natural, given the nature of corporate America today.

- *There is a potential conflict between authority/power over others and approval/acceptance.* Ultimately the vast majority of us want to be liked and approved of by others. For many people, authority threatens this need. If I want my supervisees to like me, what will happen if I need to discipline them? What if I must lead them into an unpopular course of action?

This conflict need not exist, but the typical ways of reducing it are to either wimp out as a leader, looking more to be liked than to be effective, or to act tyranically, opting for power over others and pretending not to care how they feel about you. The better way to eliminate the conflict is to become the type of leader who, like Jesus, could blend authority, friendliness, and caring.

- *Speech qualifiers.* Recent research has found that women and men express themselves differently in their speech patterns in ways that tend to enhance a man's perceived power while diminishing that of a woman. A man's speech is usually more straightforward, whereas a woman is more likely to use qualifiers such as "I think," "I feel," "I guess." The routine use of these words suggests a lack of determination and perhaps timidity or tentativeness.

These qualifiers slip into conversation unconsciously to form a speech habit. You might wish to tape-record a normal conversation with a friend and then listen for their presence.

Awareness is the first step in eliminating them. Jesus never minced words. Neither should you.

• *Nervous habits.* Nail-biting, picking at your face or hands, scratching, finger drumming, picking lint off your clothing, or other little subconscious habits undermine your power. They suggest that you are nervous or unsure of yourself, regardless of how powerfully you speak. When these occur during a conversation, they also give the impression that you are not fully listening. You will lose points in the eyes of others, and they usually will never tell you so. In fact, they may respond so subtly to these nervous habits that they themselves can't put a finger on why they lack confidence in you.

Here are some tips to help you assume your authority in the most effective manner.

• Get your mission and goals for your leadership crystal-clear in your mind, and also in your heart. Cast them into simple but powerful language which your followers will understand and which will inspire them to action, as Jesus did.

• Examine how you come across to others. Be straightforward and direct. Eliminate speech qualifiers and nervous habits. Pay attention to your dress, grooming, and overall image. Presenting an appropriate, coordinated outward image will help command respect from others, and it will help you feel more in control.

• Develop powerful body language: gestures, gait, facial expression, posture. Your body language will quickly reveal to others how well you accept your authority. Powerful people are more likely to lean forward in a conversation, with shoulders erect and hands and legs relaxed, making good eye contact. Subordinates may cast their eyes downward or lean back. When entering an executive's office, a subordinate may wait to be acknowledged, while the boss may not even knock. If you enter quickly and walk right up to the occupant's desk, you imply equal or higher status.[3] The powerful ones express through body language that they own the place, conveying a quiet air of confidence that they belong there. Jesus routinely did this, preaching and debating in the Temple and in the synagogues, starting at age twelve! Learn to use your body language to help you convey the degree of power you need in a given situation. Every situation is different. Sometimes you will want to come on strong, and at other times you will want to back off.

- Fake it till you make it. This is not to suggest dishonesty. Rather, if you feel insecure, figure out the role of a powerful leader. Try acting in that role toward your followers. If you do a good job of it, you will actually begin to become within yourself the part you are acting out. Psychotherapists use role-playing very successfully with their clients to practice new behaviors. You can do the same.

- If you've been bitten by the Imposter Phenomenon bug, work to eliminate it. Look long and hard at the positive objective realities of your successes. Focus on strengths and determine how to maximize them. Believe completely in your right and power to lead.

- Anticipate opposition. If you can figure out who is likely to oppose you and on what grounds, you can prepare a counterstrategy and rebuttal. If in your public statements you can cite and refute your opponents' arguments before they voice them, you will have added to your power and credibility.

- Consider getting a mentor (inside or outside your organization) or a career coach. A career coach is a private counselor who can help you establish goals and develop strategies, and help you manage the competitive pressures and other stresses of your job. Look for a psychologist or other mental health professional who also is highly versed in occupational issues.

- Follow the rest of the tactics in this book. Each one in its own way will make the path to positive, powerful leadership easier to climb. Jesus charted the course, and as he would say, "They that have ears to hear, let them hear. Go and do likewise."

3
EGO AND APPEAL

Now he told a parable to those who were invited, when he marked how they chose the places of honor, saying to them, "When you are invited by any one to a marriage feast, do not sit down in a place of honor, lest a more eminent man than you be invited by him; and he who invited you both will come and say to you, 'Give place to this man,' and then you will begin with shame to take the lowest place. But when you are invited, go and sit in the lowest place, so that when your host comes he may say to you, 'Friend, go up higher'; then you will be honored in the presence of all who sit at table with you. For every one who exalts himself will be humbled, and he who humbles himself will be exalted."

Luke 14:7–11

After this the Lord appointed seventy others, and sent them on ahead of him, two by two, into every town and place where he himself was about to come. . . .The seventy returned with joy, saying, "Lord, even the demons are subject to us in your name!" And he said to them, "I saw Satan fall like lightning from heaven. Behold, I have given you authority to tread upon serpents and scorpions, and over all the power of the enemy; and nothing shall hurt you. Nevertheless do not rejoice in this, that the spirits are subject to you; but rejoice that your names are written in heaven."

Luke 10:1, 17–20

In the first passage, Jesus is saying, "Don't puff yourself up or blow your own horn. Rather, display a healthy humility. Your accomplishments and position will speak for themselves. Let your honor derive from others." In the second passage, Jesus admonishes the seventy missionaries whom he sent out to get their priorities in order. Rejoicing is fine, but (1) recognize where your true source of power lies, and (2) rejoice for the right reasons.

In these selections, and in numerous others throughout the Gospels, Jesus zeroes in on Public (and Private) Enemy Number One—the ego. Spiritually aware people down through the ages have known that the ego is the primary thorn in the flesh of the spiritual life. In fact, pride has been labeled by many theologians as the original sin. What we have not learned, however, in any real, practical sense, is that the ego is the enemy of everything else worthwhile as well.

By "ego" I am referring to that side of us that yearns for self-importance, the prideful, boastful, self-aggrandizing side of our personalities. I have heard people say on numerous occasions that to hold a high-level leadership position in industry or government requires a big ego. In fact, nothing is further from the truth.

To clarify this matter, let's distinguish the ego from two other important factors. The first is the striving we all have to improve our lot. Psychiatrist Alfred Adler wrote that the main biological-social drive in nature is to grow from a minus to a plus. Every living organism does it, and so does humankind.

According to Adler, all our lives we are engaged in a striving for significance, to make our situation better. The crimes of the felon and the delusions of the schizophrenic are actually mistaken attempts to improve their situations, based on their faulty perceptions of themselves and their environment. To want to succeed, to rise, to expand our horizons, to develop our potential, to make a contribution—all this is perfectly natural and proper. It's a biological and social imperative without which "progress" could not exist. Ego, as we shall see, is actually a perversion of this drive.

The second factor is positive self-concept or self-esteem. This is a solid sense of our own intrinsic worth and a healthy, positive appreciation of our own unique talents, capabilities, assets, and limitations. High self-esteem leads to high self-acceptance, and a feeling of oneness with others, which Adler termed *Gemeinschaftsgefuhl*, or social feeling, social interest. When we examine the ego carefully, we find that the ego is actually the enemy of high self-esteem.

Self-esteem and the striving to grow and develop must be nurtured; the ego is a lion that must be muzzled and tamed. How is the ego so self-destructive?

- *The ego derives from, and actually promotes, low self-esteem.* The ego actually denies your intrinsic worth, and then creates a need and a system for compensating for that felt lack of worth. It implies that you are not acceptable as you are. Therefore, according to your ego, you must become more acceptable. We all can become "better," but "more acceptable"? To whom? The ego creates the mistaken notion that you must prove yourself to others.

  The redeemed are perfect already. What can be improved? Our behavior, our attitudes, our thinking? Yes. Our worth? Never!
- *The ego is built upon comparison.* When the ego dominates, you're not good enough until you are "*the best*" or "better than." To the ego, your worth is always relative, and can

fluctuate depending on where others stand on your ego's private measuring scale. Therefore:

- *The ego breeds competitiveness, envy, and jealousy.* All traditional competition is based on "ego needs." Competition is the outgrowth of, and leads to more, comparison. The ego spurs us into feeling envious, and therefore competitive, with those whom we deem to be superior to us. We can never be comfortable with those with whom we are competing. Therefore:

- *The ego divides people.* It encourages people to sabotage and undercut each other. It is the demon that fuels turf wars, and ethnic, racial, and sexual prejudice. The raw ego is not capable of cooperation. It knows nothing about relating as equals. It views the world in vertical terms: who's above and who's below. It is incapable of sharing and must hold the field alone. To the ego, because it believes that the best things in life are scarce, giving is losing. The ego, by definition, will clash with other egos. But since other people and their egos populate our world and cannot be avoided:

- *The ego puts the source of satisfaction outside ourselves and God.* Because our egos constantly compare and therefore make our sense of our self-worth relative to others, then certain other people become the standard-bearers or determiners of our worth. The ego must keep up with the Joneses. Therefore, emotional self-reliance is diminished. When this occurs, we can never have lasting peace, and we can never operate on a spiritual plane. When we think we've arrived, someone else can get ahead and knock us out of the top slot. So when the ego dominates, we must always be vigilant, protecting our rears lest someone sneak up on us from behind and surpass us.

- *The ego makes us dependent, and therefore vulnerable:* dependent on having our own way, upon keeping others in check or beneath us. As soon as we deem our worth to be relative, we become vulnerable to slights, put-downs, and rejection. Highly "sensitive" people are easily hurt. That is because they are allowing their egos to dominate and determine their self-esteem.

Here's the bottom line: if your ego dominates, you can't be maximally effective as a leader! You will tend to use your followers for your own purposes. You are likely to hog the credit, even if it results from the work of others. You will be tempted to mistrust your followers' motives and to suppress their development and advancement lest they ultimately surpass you. You are likely to develop a haughty, superior, or suspicious attitude which will ultimately rob you of friends and the support of your followers.

If you are ego-oriented, you are a slave to your ego. It holds you in bondage and limits your options. You are defensive because you feel a need to protect yourself and your sense of your worth. Basically the ego is founded upon, thrives on, and promotes *fear*. And fear and love cannot coexist.

Jesus is saying so much more than just to act humbly. He is saying that the ego must be tempered, reduced, eliminated. That is the only way you can be free to maximize your potential. Can anyone be truly free of the ego? Highly unlikely, but we can lessen its impact and move beyond its dictates.

The world view and perspective on life are very different for (relatively) ego-free persons than for ego-oriented people. The ego-free people are truly liberated. Self-esteem and sense of self-worth are very high. Because they know they are worthwhile as people and acceptable before God, they can be nondefensive and open, having nothing to fear. Because they have nothing they need to protect, they are invulnerable. They remain undaunted in the face of rejection, put-downs, or other negative circumstances. Their faith in their Creator and in their God-given talents is strong.

The faith of the ego-oriented person is actually weak. When faced with a challenging task, his first question is likely to be "Will I succeed or fail?" (Usually he expects to fail.) Therefore, he doubts himself and begins to worry. Because he identifies his self-worth with his performance, he is intimidated by risks and challenges. Therefore, he may limit his options to what he knows he can do well. Work becomes a problem because that's where his worth is on the line. Therefore, he will avoid risk, and will make excuses and cast blame onto others when things go wrong. Because change and ambiguity are an ego threat, he is likely to be close-minded and will try to force or manipulate the situation so as to protect himself and to get his own way. He is not likely to come up with new ideas or effectively inspire others. So much for the ego-oriented person trying to be a transformational leader!

The ego-free person has it much easier and can produce so much more! When faced with a challenge, the ego-free person first asks, "What must I do or use to accomplish the task or to solve the problem?" Because she believes her worth is given, independent of any particular performance, she can be confident and self-affirming. Such a person is free to accept—and even welcome—changes, challenges, and risk. Work is not a problem, but an opportunity to shine, to try out new ideas and activities, to succeed. Thus she is enthusiastic and creative, flexible and open-minded, because she knows that, succeed or fail, win or lose, her worth and spirit are intact, not riding on the outcome. Even more important, she is free to cooperate and will share leadership and credit with others. Unlike the ego-oriented person, the ego-free leader recognizes that if her people win, she wins, too.

For the ego-oriented person, giving is losing because it takes something away from himself. For the ego-free person, giving is expanding because now more people have and can use what was given. The world view of the ego-oriented person is scarcity, while for the ego-free person, it is abundance. The attitude of the ego-oriented person is defensive distrust, while for the ego-free person, it is open unassailableness and faith.

The ego-oriented person bogs himself down with worries about "How am I doing?" while the ego-free person focuses on

"What am I doing?" Very different issues and perspectives indeed.

Do you see, as a leader, where you need to be? None of us is truly, completely ego-free. The ego is an illusion that is supported by every facet and aspect of our society: our games, sports, schools, businesses, and even our houses of worship. Our whole social reward system is based on ego gratification, and an attempt to eschew it will often lead to wonderment and criticism from those who are still embedded in it.

How can we break free, and develop the attitude that Jesus preached and demonstrated?

1. *Look beyond the obvious, beneath the surface.* To escape the trap of the ego, we must develop the ability to see our society's fallacies, to separate out the falsehood from ultimate truth. We need to develop a wiser, more long-term spiritual understanding. So many of my counseling and consulting clients are succeeding by society's standards, yet complain of meaninglessness in their lives. We have to transcend society if we are to become truly free, and discover what really counts.

2. *Remember first and foremost where your true power lies.* Every breath we take is a gift from God. Every talent and gift we possess is a trust from the Lord. We are trustees of these gifts, and children of the Kingdom. As such, we must never forget that no matter how long or tough the road, we never walk alone. We have every right to proclaim, along with St. Paul, "I can do all things through Christ who strengthens me" (Phil. 4:13). As channels of God's power on earth, we can have incredible courage, if only we open our eyes and hearts to allow His power to work through us. If we do, we will not only be more effective leaders, we will also not get sidetracked into the self-aggrandizing traps of the ego. Prayer and spiritual development are the keys to open us to the Spirit.

3. *Develop an attitude of healthy humility.* Most of us are con-

fused about humility. While few would admit it, what most of us do to exercise "humility" is to deny our strengths and accomplishments. For example, we are uncomfortable with compliments. How often, when others lavish us with praise, do we say, "Oh, it wasn't that great"? To put ourselves down or deny our successes is an affront to God as well as to ourselves. God gave us the capability to succeed, and desires—even expects—us to succeed. Certainly self-criticism is not what a "humble attitude" is all about.

Rather, true humility is an attitude of gratitude. A feeling of thankfulness for the power and opportunity to succeed, and for the recognition that you might have received.

Of course, true humility also means keeping your priorities straight. To do something strictly for the recognition you'll get is to operate solely from the ego. The truly humble person acts because of the need of the situation. Recognition is secondary. But if it comes, he can enjoy it.

4. *Stay mission-focused rather than me-focused.* Once you focus on yourself, you lose sight of the ultimate objective. As a "competition coach" for professional athletes, I have found that if I can get them to stop worrying about *how* they're doing or what score they're getting, and keep them focused on the athletic activity itself, their performance improves. To perform at one's best in a sport—or in business and in life—the score must be irrelevant.

You have only so much energy. Any effort at ego-gratification takes away from the accomplishment of the mission. Strive to make a contribution. That's the only thing that counts. Do that, draw your gratification from that, and the recognition and all the rest will follow.

Let's get one thing straight that perhaps should have been clarified earlier. There's nothing wrong with recognition. It is one of humankind's prime motivators, and the transformational leader makes liberal and lavish use of it. The concern that we're addressing in this chapter is not with recognition per se, but with how it is derived. It should be the natural response of others to the good that you and your people have accomplished. Only then is it meaningful. If it is manufactured through false pride or manipulation, it is shallow and without substance, and will soon turn sour.

5. *Develop a clear understanding of your own strengths and limitations.* People who are hung up on mistaken humility (which is actually ego-motivated!) have a real problem admitting their strengths. To be an effective leader, however, you must not only know them inside and out, but enjoy them as well. Then you can develop them and use them freely. After all, you *can't* develop or improve what you don't see, and you *won't* improve what you don't enjoy! If you don't believe this, just try to get a seven-year old who'd rather be playing baseball to practice his violin!

   Why have a clear view of your limitations? To "keep you humble"? Hardly. It's useful to know that you can't do everything, but much more important, by knowing your limitations, it's easier to plan how to overcome or use them, or to select others for your team to fill that gap and complement your talents (see Chapter 7).

6. *Make it your life's policy to give more than you get.* I once knew a person who was a security guard at a local supermarket. He was disgusted with his job, with his status, and with his pay. He stated that he admired Mother Teresa, whereupon he got the idea that if he wanted to solve his job problem, he should model himself on his job after her. He did so, and at Christmas he received over a dozen cards from customers at the market. Now, who in the world would write a Christmas card to the store security guard unless he made a significant impact in some small way on one's life? A word of warning: giving more than you get becomes increasingly difficult in a world of faith, based on the principle of abundance!

7. *Learn to laugh at yourself.* The ego drives us to take ourselves so seriously, to be so perfectionistic, and therefore gets threatened by jokes at our expense. No one enjoys a

hurtful attack veiled in humor, but good clean fun is no threat. If we learn to see and accept our imperfections as part of our unique character, like distress marks which add to the value of certain antique furniture, then we have a much healthier outlook, and a stronger self-esteem. One who can laugh at oneself is truly invulnerable.

To close with a brief example: John is the vice president of marketing for a large firm. He sends a newsletter throughout the company to make other employees aware of what the marketing department has accomplished. In that newsletter and publicly at meetings and awards ceremonies, he highlights the accomplishments of his people. Never does he appear to be the star. When asked about it, he said, "My people would do anything I ask. They'll go the extra mile for me anytime. The president knows that ultimately I'm responsible for what my division accomplishes. That's enough for me. My happy and productive staff—that's what makes me possible."

Need we say more?

4
WHO'S WHO? SETTING THE EXAMPLE

But Jesus called [the disciples] to him and said, "You know that the rulers of the Gentiles lord it over them, and their great men exercise authority over them. It shall not be so among you; but whoever would be great among you must be your servant, and whoever would be first among you must be your slave; even as the Son of man came not to be served but to serve, and to give his life as a ransom for many."

Matt. 20:25–28
(*Parallel texts:* Mark 10:42–45; Luke 22:24–26)

[Jesus] rose from supper, laid aside his garments, and girded himself with a towel. Then he poured water into a basin, and began to wash the disciples' feet, and to wipe them with the towel with which he was girded. . . . When he had washed their feet, and taken his garments, and resumed his place, he said to them, "Do you know what I have done to you? You call me Teacher and Lord; and you are right, for so I am. If I then, your Lord and Teacher, have

> washed your feet, you also ought to wash one another's
> feet."
>
> John 13:4–5, 12–14
>
> (*Parallel text:* Luke 22:27)

Ah, the old ego rises again. The mother of disciples James
and John approached Jesus, asking that her two sons might sit
at Jesus' right and left hand in the Kingdom. At this, the other
disciples became indignant. This situation sparked Jesus'
words in the Matthew passage above.

The preceding passage from John occurred at the Last Supper. Luke's account of the Last Supper includes an account of
a dispute among the disciples as to "which of them was to be
regarded as the greatest" (Luke 22:24b). It may well have been
in the aftermath of that dispute that Jesus felt it necessary to
give his disciples an object lesson by washing their feet.

In the rock opera *Jesus Christ Superstar*,[1] while Jesus is in
lament at the Last Supper, the disciples are singing about always wanting to be apostles and knowing that they could make
it if they tried hard enough. Then they could retire and write a
Gospel so that the world would remember them after they've
died.

Power. Glory. Fame. Fine things in and of themselves, but
what red herrings they can be. So quickly they can go to our
heads. When that happens, empowered leadership becomes
perverted, and subverted. Again the old ego often makes it difficult for the leader to keep priorities straight.

In word and symbol, as well as in his everyday actions, Jesus
set an example of the servant leader. Jesus often referred to
himself as a shepherd. At first this may seem a simple analogy,
but it is actually a complex role:

• The shepherd guides and directs the sheep. He determines
  where to graze, where to take the flock. He charts the course
  and determines whether and how far to move the flock on any
  given day.

- The shepherd protects the flock. He guards the sheepfold at night to keep out poachers or animals that could do the sheep harm. He pursues strays so that they are not lost or fall into danger.
- The shepherd anticipates and meets the sheep's needs. He knows how much food they need to consume, so he leads them into adequate grazing pasture rather than into barren or sparse land. He makes sure that his resources, such as quality and number of assistants and sheepdogs, are adequate for the size of the flock.

So we see that not only does a shepherd lead the flock, he also serves it. Why? Because it's his job, but also for another reason:

- The shepherd loves the sheep. It is his caring for the flock that fuels his willingness to fight rather than run when the flock is in danger, and to risk life and limb to protect them (see Luke 15:3, 7; John 10:1–6).

Clearly, as Jesus implies from his use of the shepherd symbol, sheepherding was not a job, but a calling. The same is true for those who are entrusted with shepherding a human flock. Those who see leadership as strictly a job will shrink from danger. They will play CYA and cast blame elsewhere rather than stand up for their followers. They will gladly garner the glory, but will hide from the dirty work or thankless tasks. In modern jargon, the latter often falls under the rubric of "delegation."

Servant leaders are truly committed. Honest caring and concern for the followers drive their daily activities.

Who is the shepherd's boss? The owner of the flock, who pays his salary . . . or the sheep? Who's your boss?

Forget the organizational chart for a minute. Let's look at "boss" from a practical point of view. The boss is the one who directs your activities, right? Admittedly, you owe your boss your allegiance and dedication. To whom, according to this definition, should it be primarily given?

Transformational leaders, like good shepherds, have no illusions about this. Their primary "bosses" are their followers, their "sheep." They understand that, in spite of job descriptions, their actual leadership role and function are defined and determined by the needs of their followers. The formal organizational role is really an abstraction, and may even have little or no bearing on nitty-gritty daily life in the trenches.

You want power, glory, fame? These derive only from *service*. This is where the rubber meets the road. Government exists by consent of the governed. That's it. That is the only operational political principle that works over the long haul. No political regime in history—nor leader—which has violated that principle has survived. Provide caring and consistently excellent service, and the personal benefits will follow.

For whom does your organization exist? For the owner or stockholders? Or for your employees, customers, or clients? Regardless of what others think, you need to be vitally clear on this issue for yourself. If Jesus were on earth today, he would definitely favor a "customer-driven" management approach. "Customer service," today's new buzzword, is actually two thousand years old! He would undoubtedly favor a "reverse pyramid" organizational structure, where the real purpose of management is to provide the proper resources to the employees—those who must make the product or serve the customer, who, in reality, is the ultimate boss.

It's so easy to act as if the followers are there to serve you. If that's the case, Jesus would say you've got it all backward. How can you develop a servant-leader approach? Many books have been written on customer service and effective leadership. The following hints, therefore, are far from exhaustive, but will get you started.

- Get your priorities straight about your purpose, your role, and who your "boss" is. You *can't act* like a servant leader until you *think* like one. Make your followers your prime concern, number one on your values list. Only then can you honestly treat your followers with the respect and dignity they deserve—the respect you would accord to your "boss."

- Stop, look, and listen. Leaders who expect to be served *perceive* differently than servant leaders do. The former rarely stop long enough to consider what their followers need, so concerned are they with their own desires.

    Servant leaders ask, and then listen. They take time to discover what their followers need, and then look for ways to fill those needs. "Listening" doesn't mean saying, "I understand." It means doing something to redress the grievance, provide support, or enable your followers to perform better. Only then can you learn to *anticipate* their future needs.

- Take your followers' emotional and spiritual needs into account as well as their physical and occupational ones. Take time to understand your followers as unique persons, learning each one's special talents, skills, limitations, goals, and dreams. Only then can you most effectively empower them. Most leaders who want to be served won't take time for this. They see it as a waste of valuable energy, whereas the servant leader views such time and energy as an investment in the good of the whole. The servant leader sees individual beauty, whereas to leaders who want to be served, most followers look alike.

- Be a good role model. Your followers will identify with you. This was Jesus' point when he washed the disciples' feet. Act out in your own life the style you wish your followers to adopt. When I was a child, my father, sometimes jokingly, would say to me, "Do as I say, don't do as I do." That approach won't cut it, but too many would-be leaders center their management philosophy around it. Don't you get caught in that trap, or you can kiss your credibility goodbye.

- Prepare to serve. Actively develop your need-meeting abilities: listening, counseling, and communication skills, as well as additional technical skills you might need. Remember that meeting human needs is a multidimensional process. Remember, too, that you increase your power to the degree that you empower.

Servant leadership. When the task is to get things done through others, does any other leadership model make sense?

5
ON COMPROMISE

Then Jesus was led up by the Spirit into the wilderness to be tempted by the devil. And he fasted forty days and forty nights, and afterward he was hungry. And the tempter came and said to him, "If you are the son of God, command these stones to become loaves of bread." But he answered, "It is written, 'Man shall not live by bread alone, but by every word that proceeds from the mouth of God.'" Then the devil took him to the holy city, and set him on the pinnacle of the temple, and said to him, "If you are the son of God, throw yourself down; for it is written, 'He will give his angels charge of you,' and 'On their hands they will bear you up, lest you strike your foot against a stone.'" Jesus said to him, "Again it is written, 'You shall not tempt the Lord your God.'" Again, the devil took him to a very high mountain, and showed him all the kingdoms of the world and the glory of them; and he said to him, "All these I will give you, if you will fall down and worship me." Then Jesus said to him, "Begone, Satan! For it is written, 'You shall worship

the Lord your God and him only shall you serve.' " Then
the devil left him, and behold, angels came and ministered to him.

Matt. 4:1–11

(*Parallel texts:* Mark 1:12, 13; Luke 4:1–13)

Before entering our discussion, a note is in order about interpretation. The English word used for the devil's activity is
tempt. This word uniformly has the connotation of leading or
enticing someone to do evil, to sin. The actual Greek word which
has been translated as "to tempt" is *peirazein*, which really
means "to test" in the sense of "test one's mettle," to see if one
can bear up under pressure, to make one stronger through trial.
In Jesus' experience in the wilderness, the devil was testing Jesus to see if he would remain true to God and his mission. The
devil wasn't really trying to encourage Jesus to sin, but rather he
wanted Jesus to compromise himself and the use of his powers.
Let's look at each test and discover what was really going on.

Jesus had been fasting under the hot desert sun for forty days.
He must have been absolutely famished and in a weakened
condition. The devil reminded Jesus that if he wanted to, he
could change the stones that were lying there into bread. The
devil added a challenge to Jesus' ego: "*If* you really are the son
of God . . ." In other words, the devil was saying, "Prove you
are who you say you are." Jesus didn't fall for it, however. He
responded by quoting Deuteronomy 8:3, "Man shall not live by
bread alone . . ."

In this and the remaining two tests, two issues are involved.
The first is the actions the devil wanted Jesus to take, simple
things for Jesus to accomplish which in and of themselves would
have been no big deal. Much more important was the second issue, the power relationship between Jesus and the devil. In
short, Jesus' testing in the wilderness was a power contest.

In the first test, there would have been no sin in Jesus' turning
stones into bread. This would have been a harmless act, and certainly Jesus needed the sustenance the bread would have pro-

vided. The symbolism involved is another matter. Jesus was being challenged to use his powers for self-serving purposes. Jesus had not yet begun his public ministry. If he were to use his powers to save or help himself there in the desert when he was alone, he might be tempted to do the same in public. After all, when one yields once, it's always easier to yield a second time, and even easier yet to give in a third time. The devil was trying to get Jesus to *establish a precedent* for self-serving behavior.

Back now to the power contest. Had Jesus turned the stones to bread, he would have done so at the devil's bidding. In power terms, if I can get you to do something you had not planned to do, then at that moment, I am in control. I have more power than you because I have influenced you. This is very subtle, but it is the feeling with which we are in touch at an emotional level whenever we resist another person's suggestions or attempts to influence us. Had Jesus given in, the devil would have had power over Jesus by influencing Jesus' behavior.

The devil was no fool. He challenged Jesus at two levels of need. The first was the intense physical need Jesus had for food. After fasting for forty days, that should have been cause enough for Jesus to give in. But the devil also tried to hook Jesus' ego. "Prove it," he was saying. "Show me." The devil threw down the gauntlet. How tempting it would have been to respond, "I'll show you." The devil knew that once a person's ego is hooked, that person may well show off by doing foolish things that later he or she would regret. Instead, Jesus remained steadfast by quoting Scripture. He held firm to a basic scriptural principle.

In the second trial, Satan tried to get Jesus to shortcut his method of demonstrating his Messiahship. Popular legend of the time held that the Messiah could hurl himself from the pinnacle of the Temple and remain unharmed. To confirm the legend would clearly demonstrate that Jesus was the Messiah. Why should Satan want Jesus to prove that?

Again, if Jesus did what the devil suggested, who would have the *real* power? But this temptation was more insidious. Jesus' mission was to demonstrate his Messiahship at a spiritual level, through his redeeming death and Resurrection. The devil wanted Jesus to "prove" it by conforming to people's expectations, and doing what amounted to a magic trick. Jesus performed many miracles, signs, and wonders, but they were always done to help others in some specific way. They were not done solely to prove a point, as hurling himself from the pinnacle of the Temple would have been. Satan's goal in this temptation was to lure Jesus off track, to take the easy way out. Again, Jesus prevailed by refusing to get hooked. How? Again by reiterating scriptural principle. Jesus knew his mission and how it was to be carried out.

The third test was like the second, also designed to lead Jesus astray. Again an ego appeal was made, but in a different way. "I'll make you rich and famous, Jesus," Satan was saying, "if you'll only do one small thing—worship me." Here again, Satan was trying to dissuade Jesus from the cross and true spiritual victory by promising to set him up as a temporal ruler. Satan may have guessed that if Jesus would betray God by violating the First Commandment, God's plan of Redemption through Jesus would be ruined. Satan was saying, in effect, "Why go the hard way of the cross to win mankind to yourself? I'll give it all to you right now!" What a choice! Be ruler of the world or die a horrible death on the cross. Which would you or I choose?

Many spiritual lessons can be learned from this account, but what is Jesus demonstrating about power to help us be effective leaders?

- Jesus was absolutely clear about his mission and how it was to be carried out. If he were not certain about his role, the tests would have been much harder to resist.
- Jesus protected himself and resisted temptation by remaining steadfast to his God and to his principles. He quoted Scripture, perhaps because this is the one thing that could stop Satan in his tracks, one thing that Satan could not refute.

These are the main lessons for us. How can we protect ourselves in the time of trial?

Determine what is compromisable and what is not. This is a vital, and perhaps difficult, distinction to make. Actions take on symbolic meanings and reflect back to your basic values. Jesus may have conceded little things, but he never jeopardized his basic values or purpose. Think through the ultimate ramifications of what you are asked to compromise.

This subtle distinction is particularly important if, like Jesus, the one trying to get you to compromise is your opponent. In corporate settings, who your opponent is may not be readily apparent. Perhaps someone is working behind the scenes, trying to set you up for a fall. If that person can get you to compromise unwisely, you might make yourself vulnerable to further difficulty. We learned in Jesus' temptation experience that little things mean a lot, and even a tiny slip could sometimes have disastrous results.

While you are more than what you do, in most people's eyes what you do determines what you are. Never forget that you are judged not as much by your successes as you are by your consistency and honesty. People will more readily trust and follow one who is consistent than they will follow a highly successful person who is erratic. Erratic people are ultimately perceived either as weak or as a threat. Either way, their credibility is damaged.

This does not mean that you should never deviate nor change your mind. People need to keep on top of new trends and make changes accordingly. Beware, however, of making changes for the wrong reasons, for example, change for change's sake, or change based on ego needs, such as being the first, or keeping up with the Joneses.

Jesus' actions demonstrate the centrality of mission and basic principles. These were his touchstone, and should be ours. Only when you are solid-rock-sure of what your mission and guiding principles and values are, can you effectively evaluate your actions. Think through the impact a particular decision will have on (1) your value system, (2) your ultimate objectives, and (3) your position as leader in terms of the role itself and how you are perceived by others. Will what you do undermine or strengthen your position? Will it enhance or destroy your credibility or others' respect for you?

These are tough times, presenting tough choices. Sometimes there is no positive solution: the best choice may just be the one that does the least damage. Sometimes as a conscientious leader, you must lead the charge. Other times you must refuse to participate. Either way, you make yourself vulnerable.

Remember, however, that the most powerful person of all, and the most unassailable, is the man or woman who remains true to high principles. By remaining steadfast, Jesus defeated Satan. By holding firmly to your principles, you may open yourself to attack, but you will also outshine the opposition and have the best opportunity to ultimately rise above. You may be defeated by others; you can leave the others behind. You cannot, however, hide from yourself. You are your constant companion. Whatever you do, you must live with yourself afterward. Succeed or fail, win or lose, when you look in the mirror, may you always come face-to-face with a man or woman of honor. You—and your followers—deserve nothing less. They can take your job; they can take your possessions. They can even take your life. But no one can strip you of your honor. Only you can do that.

Keep your ego in line. Never let it eclipse your basic principles if you can help it. Recognize in yourself your ego tendencies so that when faced with a tough choice, you can sort out the issues and your motivations. Remember that your ego is a red herring and that you will ultimately gain more by being true to your guiding principles than if you allow your ego to sidetrack you.

When faced with tough trials and temptations, follow Jesus' example. Let your conscience and your mission be your guide, and by all means, play by the Book.

6
DEAL DIRECTLY

On the third day there was a marriage at Cana in Galilee, and the mother of Jesus was there; Jesus also was invited to the marriage, with his disciples. When the wine failed, the mother of Jesus said to him, "They have no wine." And Jesus said to her, "O woman, what have you to do with me? My hour has not yet come." His mother said to the servants, "Do whatever he tells you." Now six stone jars were standing there, for the Jewish rites of purification, each holding twenty or thirty gallons. Jesus said to them, "Fill the jars with water." And they filled them up to the brim. He said to them, "Now draw some out, and take it to the steward of the feast." So they took it. When the steward of the feast tasted the water now become wine, and did not know where it came from (though the servants who had drawn the water knew), the steward of the feast called the bridegroom and said to him, "Every man serves the good wine first; and when men have drunk freely, then the poor wine; but you have kept the good wine until now."

John 2:1–10

In comparison to Jesus' other feats, changing water into wine was a minor miracle, and it has perhaps become one of his most famous ones. This story has been the subject of countless sermons and has been interpreted thousands of times in hundreds of ways for its deeper spiritual meaning.

For our purposes, let's look at what actually happened. Cana in Galilee was a little backwater town, very close to Nazareth, where Jesus grew up, practicing the carpenter's trade with his father, Joseph. Jesus' mother was invited, along with Jesus and his disciples. Mary was probably a very close friend or even a relative of the parents of the groom, for she seemed to have some authority to command the servants.

In Jesus' day, hospitality was very important at all levels of social class. There were strict traditions and social codes attached to such events as weddings. The feasting and well-wishing would last for several days. To throw a wedding was a costly endeavor, especially for working-class folk, so a great deal of "status" was involved in doing it properly and abundantly, even more so than would be the case today. If any of the provisions, especially the wine, were to run out, that would be a social faux pas of the highest order and would bring absolute, shameful disgrace down upon the heads of the newlyweds and the groom's parents.

Jesus' act, then, was one of tender compassion. He bailed out his friends and family. He cared enough to get involved. What and why Jesus did what he did are instructive, but our greatest lessons derive from *how* he did it.

1. It wasn't his business, or his problem. There is no direct implication from Mary's statement, "They have no wine," that she expected Jesus to intervene. Certainly she would have been concerned for the host, but that could have been the extent of it. But hearing this news, Jesus *felt a responsibility* to intervene, even though it was, for all practical purposes, not his concern. Jesus' desire to rectify the situation was undoubtedly based on his caring for the people involved and the situation as a whole.

   Many years ago Henry Ford stated that the way to create a

successful business was to "find a need and fill it." The transformational leader must, therefore, never play the ostrich, head buried in the sand of his or her own function or sphere of influence. Rather the leader must be ready to step in however and wherever the need might arise. Keep your eyes and ears open, always ready for the unexpected.

2. Jesus didn't hesitate. He stepped right in. Was this impulsive acting out on his part? No way. He knew his options, and the extent of his power. He knew what he would be able to accomplish, and he went about it in an orderly fashion.

So often, fools rush in. Yet in an emergency situation you don't always have time to run it by a committee or wait for consensus. Therefore, it's critical for the leader to have done his or her homework in advance. Have a firm understanding of your own strengths, capabilities, and power, and how you fit into the broader picture. Thus prepared, you can jump into the fray when an emergency arises, confident that you can succeed.

3. Jesus didn't take time to explain himself. He acted quickly, but also gently. The Greek words that are translated "Woman, what have you to do with me?" sound very harsh and cutting in English, but that is not how those words were meant. A better translation might be "Mom, trust me. What I'm about to do is beyond your understanding, but leave it to me. I'll handle the situation in my own way."

So often, explanations slow us down. A prime political stall tactic is to bog everything down in paperwork, in proposals and defense. Jesus had the guts to act instinctively, bypassing rhetoric. How many opportunities have you seen slip away because of "analysis paralysis"? Enough said. Sometimes you have to act on instinct. There's plenty of time for talk afterward.

4. Jesus dealt directly with the people involved. He worked one on one with the servants, bypassing their boss, the steward of the feast. He ignored the chain of command. You

notice he didn't go to the steward and instruct the steward to command the servants. He commanded them himself. If Jesus had any concern as to whether the steward would feel his authority threatened, or that he might feel that Jesus was an interloper, sticking his nose into the steward's business, Jesus also knew that when he was through, the steward and the host would look like heroes.

Jesus got away with breeching protocol. But you had better watch out! It is considered a cardinal sin to go over your boss's head, or to take command of another boss's employees. Sometimes, however, the need is so great that the risk is worth it. This is why it is so critical to have made a careful assessment early on as to how far you can flex your political muscle. If we look around us honestly, most corporate crucifixions are, like Jesus' was, not based on actual incompetence, wrongdoing, or failed performance, but upon political "expediency." If you must take matters into your own hands, be prepared to smooth the way as you go whenever possible. Just as important as solving the problem is allowing those involved to save face.

5. Jesus let the steward and the bridegroom take the credit. In the story, the steward had no idea what happened. Neither did the bridegroom. But everyone came out a winner.

Jesus performed his miracle in the back room. There was no public display, no ostentation, no attempt to overshadow the host. Jesus had no need to make his action public; word would spread soon enough. In the meantime, the guests, knowing nothing of the wine situation, would continue to enjoy themselves, and the party would be saved.

In Chapter 3, we spoke about the role of the ego. Here is another example. If Jesus wanted any ultimate publicity about his identity, he was able to trust those servants to spread the word in their own way. Likewise you need to trust the same basic principle. The word of your successful intervention will spread. This does not mean, however, that sometimes, for political purposes, it isn't wise to help that word spread by a well-placed memo or two. But the main notice and praise should come from those whom you have helped.

Here's another key point: Jesus really didn't usurp anyone else's authority. He saw the need and was able to move right in. However, you need to be careful about overstepping bounds. You might see a need, but it might be hedged in with political fences, making direct access impossible. If you cross those fences, you must do so in a way that makes those upon whose territory you step come up smelling like a rose. Often this won't be easy, but to do so is imperative if at all possible. The last thing you need is to turn others' turf into enemy territory. If you feel you must act in a difficult political situation, shore up your alliances, and get the proper support if time permits.

Weighing need against political pressure is often a difficult choice. For the transformational leader, however, need usually wins. Handled adroitly, the intervention won't raise too many political hackles, and will, hopefully, come out to everyone's benefit.

Sometimes, however, need and politics can't be reconciled. In another situation, Jesus was criticized by the Pharisees for healing a man on the Sabbath, which technically was against the Sabbath law. Jesus made no apology, but stated, "The Sabbath was made for man, not man for the Sabbath."

Jesus had his priorities in order. So must you. It's never easy when politics work against human need. Here is where you must choose. At the wedding in Cana, politics was not a problem. But regardless, the principles that the story illustrates remain the same.

As a leader, you set the pace and establish the standard, not only for your followers but for others involved as well. Let that standard be one of action, of courage, and of caring, empowered by the Spirit.

7
HANG AROUND THE DOCKS

As he walked by the Sea of Galilee, he saw two brothers, Simon who is called Peter and Andrew his brother, casting a net into the sea; for they were fishermen. And he said to them, "Follow me, and I will make you fishers of men." Immediately they left their nets and followed him. And going on from there he saw two other brothers, James the son of Zebedee and John his brother, in the boat with Zebedee their father, mending their nets, and he called them. Immediately they left the boat and their father, and followed him.

Matt. 4:18–22

(*Parallel text:* Mark 1:16–20)

After this he went out, and saw a tax collector, named Levi, sitting at the tax office; and he said to him, "Follow me." And he left everything, and rose and followed him.

Luke 5:27, 28

(*Parallel texts:* Matt. 9:9; Mark 2:13, 14)

The names of the twelve apostles are these: first, Simon, who is called Peter, and Andrew his brother; James the son of Zebedee, and John his brother; Philip and Bartholomew; Thomas and Matthew the tax collector; James the son of Alphaeus, and Thaddaeus; Simon the Cananaean, and Judas Iscariot, who betrayed him.

Matt. 10:2–4

(*Parallel texts:* Mark 3:14–19; Luke 6:13–16)

What a motley crew! Was Jesus out of his head to select such a bunch? At least four of them were commercial fishermen. One was probably a crook, and another may well have been a political assassin. Let's look at his choices more carefully.

Fishing in Jesus' day was definitely a blue-collar trade, one with a long past and no future. Once a fisherman, always a fisherman. One did not enter that trade to "get ahead." Most likely, they were poorly schooled. They were physically strong, but probably a coarse lot. Most commercial fishing in that day was done by family businesses. Father passed the trade onto his sons, who in turn would pass the skills on to the next generation. Undoubtedly there was close family togetherness and pride among fisherfolk. For Peter, Andrew, James, and John to drop their nets and to follow Jesus was therefore much more than an abrupt career change. It meant turning their backs on, and perhaps letting down, their blood kin.

Matthew (Levi) was no apparent prize. He was a tax collector. In Jesus' day, tax collectors were appointed by Rome. Most of them were themselves members of the subjugated peoples who obtained their positions by volunteering for them. Once approved, they had Rome's full backing. They made their living by assessing a surcharge, or commission, to the regular taxes. Since there were so many taxes and people usually did not know how much the various taxes really were, excesses and extortion were commonplace. Many tax collectors cheated the public and the government alike, took bribes, and grew quite wealthy.

While most of us are not particularly fond of the IRS, tax collectors in Jesus' Palestine were despised. They were viewed as turncoats who exploited their own kith and kin, turning over the people's hard-earned money to the coffers of their captors. As a result, tax collectors were social and religious outcasts, regarded a little below the harlots, thieves, and murderers. They were not permitted to enter the synagogues, nor could their testimony be accepted in civil courts. Jesus was sorely criticized for befriending and eating with tax collectors.

Simon the Cananaean could also have been a hot potato. In the Gospel of Luke, Simon was referred to as a Zealot. The Zealots were a radical, nationalistic political faction whose main purpose was the overthrow of Rome. In fact, among the Zealots was an inner circle of dagger men called the Sicarii. These were cutthroat political assassins, much like undercover guerrilla terrorists of our day.

What was Jesus up to? His choice of disciples offended some of the religious leaders. But Jesus wanted to carry on a religious ministry. Shouldn't he have chosen followers of influence, powerful members of the religious establishment? Wouldn't his ministry have had more clout if he were politically well connected? We do know from the Gospels that Jesus attracted somewhat of a following from the rich and influential, for example, Nicodemus the Pharisee and Joseph of Arimathea, who donated his tomb for Jesus' body. Yet he apparently chose his disciples for different reasons.

What did Jesus need? People he could train, who would readily believe and accept his point of view, whom he could send out across the country to further his mission. Jesus' call meant a career change for his disciples into a profession with little financial benefit and constant travel. Would the politically or financially connected persons be ready to take on that kind of occupation? Hardly.

Jesus apparently saw in these men something they did not see in themselves—their potential to expand beyond their immediate horizons. They became preachers, administrators, social workers, healers, and in the case of several, authors.

Jesus looked beneath the surface. In Simon the fisherman he

saw a stalwart personality, and renamed him Peter, which means "rock." In John, he must have seen a tremendous personal sensitivity and empathy. In Matthew, he probably saw a talent for figures and writing. In "doubting Thomas" he probably saw a conservative, thoughtful attitude which could bring balance to the brashness of Peter and perhaps Simon the Zealot.

Bible scholar William Barclay offers a fascinating insight into a possible reason Jesus chose the fishermen to become the "fishers of men." Good fishermen must have *patience*. Catching fish and winning people over takes time. They must also have *courage*. As fishermen faced danger on the sea, the disciples faced dangers in telling people the truth. They must also have *perseverance*. Fishermen and preachers must never get discouraged, but always must be willing to try again. They must have *an eye for the right moment*. As a good fisherman senses when it is a good time to fish, the wise preacher and teacher chooses the right moment to make contact. He must *fit the bait to the fish*. As the fisherman must select the proper bait, the teacher must learn under what conditions and with whom he or she can work best. The wise fisherman must *keep himself out of sight*. If the fish spot him, they won't bite. Likewise, Jesus needed people who would not go off on an ego trip, but who could present Jesus' message of the Kingdom of God without getting themselves in the way.[1]

In making his choice of disciples, Jesus ignored public convention, social pressure, and power politics. He chose based on the potential within the disciples themselves, not on the secondary issues of influence. He had a clear understanding of his priorities.

Jesus chose, but why did they follow? They all had stable careers. Why did they lay them down instantly and just walk away with Jesus? Were they all unhappy, dissatisfied, and longing for escape? Were they adventure seekers or would-be soldiers of fortune? Highly doubtful.

Jesus is a study in transformational leadership. Look at his technique. Instantly, in the same breath as his call, he made them a promise and showed them a vision in terms they could readily understand: "Follow me, and I will make you fishers of men." Here is the challenge—to reach out to accomplish something new, something more than they had dreamed possible—and Jesus promised to empower them to do it. So simple, yet so dramatically powerful.

Jesus approached them with a command that implied a sense of urgency. He didn't say, "Hey, Simon, I'm thinking that you might make a good disciple. Would you consider joining up with me? Think it over a couple of days and let's get back in touch." Simple, powerful, and straightforward. Take it or leave it. That was Jesus' tactic.

Jesus also made them feel needed and important. His call conveyed a special role which captured their imaginations and gave them a unique position. They must have sensed that they would become a vital link in Jesus' overall mission. In his own way, he answered the basic question we all would eventually ask if confronted with a similar offer: "What's in it for me?"

Harking back to Chapter 2, Jesus called his disciples with a tone and sense of authority: "I want you, and here's what I'm going to enable you to do." No question, no hesitation, total certainty.

There are numerous tips embedded here that can help us in picking our associates or others who must work with or under us:

- Focus on what you need to get the job done. Identify the skills and talents you need in your key people or other workers.
- Look beyond the obvious. Don't evaluate people just based on their outward accomplishments up to this point. Rather, consider their inner potential. It's not what they have done before, but what they can do for you now and in the future that really counts.
- Don't ignore the rejects. Certain people with hidden talents never get picked, so they never have a chance to shine. Don't assume that because others have overlooked or rejected these

people, they have nothing to offer. They may have been by-passed for political or superficial reasons. Such people can be a treasure trove of latent talent, and may even work all the harder for you because you gave them a chance.

- Choose for strength. Insecure leaders fear strength in their subordinates and key associates, while truly powerful leaders applaud and nurture it. The stronger your subordinates, if they are loyal, the more your team will accomplish and the better you, as the manager, will look.

For many managers, picking subordinates is like playing limbo. The manager, through his or her own capabilities, sets the standards of performance, and everyone else must work below that level. To try to make yourself indispensable by selecting associates who are less competent than you are is sheer folly, and may actually impede your chances of advancement. If your superiors see that your unit can't function without you, they won't risk promoting you. If you build a temple to yourself at work, you are likely to be buried in it.

- Choose for diversity; foster and reward it. Your people must be loyal and able to work together. Beyond that, diversity reigns. Choose people whose skills complement each other and yours. By so doing, you expand the overall capabilities of your unit. In fact, people with diverse roles may work together better than people with the same duties and talents, because their own special uniqueness can reduce their threat, add to their perceived importance, and may therefore reduce internal competitiveness.

Often mahogany row is a study in imitation. Unfortunately, managers attempt to clone themselves through their subordinates. While they would deny this, it often becomes obvious when the key people act, think, and talk like the boss, or have basically the same talents as the boss. Bosses who thus attempt to clone themselves want peace and an easy road.

Inwardly they are insecure and fear conflict, so they nurture and reward imitation and subtly discourage diversity. They perceive diversity as unsafe.

In reality, only *unmanaged* diversity is a threat. Well-managed diversity benefits everyone. It keeps people on their toes, brings out fresh ideas, fosters creativity, and raises exciting challenges. Yes, it can also lead to more conflict, but conflict among people who care about the overall mission and about each other can lead to new opportunities. Consider such conflict a resource.

Naturally it's harder to hold the reins on a spirited horse than on a docile one, but you will get a faster and more exciting ride!

- Watch out for the "safe" ones. Sometimes those noncontroversial people whom everyone would consider a safe bet earned that reputation by not taking risks or doing anything truly worthwhile. Rather you want people who are willing to risk criticism for the sake of their ideas, innovation, or your mission. "Safe" people remain so by limiting themselves, and if your team members limit themselves, they limit you!

- Look in unusual places. Don't be afraid to stray from the normal channels for picking your associates. If the janitor possesses certain skills, talents, or insights you need, why not select him? Leave no stone unturned. Your ultimate goal is to find the right people with the right combination of talents to best fulfill your mission and objectives. Often these people can best be located in unconventional situations. To stick strictly to protocol can close the door to undiscovered opportunities.

In which strange places should you look? Ask yourself what you need, and what kinds of people have those talents and skills. Then ask yourself where you most likely will find such people. Check around, and don't be too hasty in coming to a decision.

- Be careful about selecting powerful and influential people. It's great if you can have people with clout on your team, but don't use political power as your primary criterion for membership. In fact, sometimes such people can become a problem. They may avoid taking a necessary stand or risk for the sake of maintaining their influence. Also they may want to excessively influence or control you. If you get lulled into making a choice based on what you feel these people can do *for* you, you may end up having to contend with what they do *to* you. Before selecting political heavy hitters, make sure of their loyalty and commitment to you, your ideas, and your goals, and be sure there are no conflicts of interest.

- Let your actual call reflect your authority and power. Simple, short, and to the point. Tell them, "Here's what I'm doing. Here's what I need. You're the person for the job, and here's why."

- Make them feel special and important. People want to know what they're going to get out of it. Recognition is a universal motivator, more powerful than perks or money. Let them know at the outset how vital their role is in the overall effort, openly recognizing their unique talents and potential contribution.

- Give them a challenge. Present them with an occasion to which to rise. By offering a challenging task, you not only capture their desire to achieve, but you also express your faith in their ability to meet or exceed it.

- Capture their imagination. Give them a vision. Appeal to their spirit of adventure and excitement, but not to their desire to have fun. There will be fun moments, but an appeal primarily to pleasure encourages them to poop out when the fun stops. A worthwhile task will have rough spots on the path, and tough obstacles to face. This makes the task all the more adventuresome. Forewarning them can add to the thrill of the enterprise.

Never forget, however, that the motives of adventure and excitement are also short-lived. Your potential followers need to feel a sense of awe and imagination in relation to the overall mission and ultimate objectives themselves, as well as to the process of achieving them. Jesus' disciples were challenged with going head to head with the political and religious establishment and turning the world upside down. Few mandates today can compete with that. But if you can challenge your people with a vision and task of great magnitude, you will capture their spirit and build strong loyalty.

Spirit fuels endeavor.
Diversity without division is divine.

8
"WHO IS MY BROTHER?"

And his mother and his brothers came; and standing outside they sent to him and called him. And a crowd was
sitting about him; and they said to him, "Your mother and
your brothers are outside, asking for you." And he replied,
"Who are my mother and my brothers?" And looking
around on those who sat about him, he said, "Here are my
mother and my brothers! Whoever does the will of God is
my brother, and sister, and mother."

Mark 3:31–35

(*Parallel texts:* Matt. 12:46–50; Luke 8:19–21)

An old TV commercial once stated, "Treat your family like
company, and your company like family." What sage advice.
Why? No feeling is stronger than family feeling, a feeling of
belonging and acceptance. A feeling that you are an integral,
vital part of something. Few moments bring greater joy than
when a family is having a happy, meaningful time together.

Likewise, few things can hurt as much as facing rejection
from a family member. We can accept it from strangers and

acquaintances much more easily. But when a close friend or family member plunges in the proverbial knife, the pain is deep indeed. That is because we have special expectations from family members. Sure, we squabble at times, but underneath there is supposed to be a special bond of love, loyalty, and caring. A bond that accepts us as we are, with all our faults, so that we don't have to prove ourselves. Our worth should be accepted without question in a family.

A healthy family promotes an "all-for-one, one-for-all" feeling. Unity and backup support, with a commitment that implies I'd climb the highest mountain, swim the deepest ocean for you, my brother/sister. With that sense of unity comes the feeling that no outside force could come between us or break us up, that we can withstand any attack as long as we have each other. Remember the line from the old song, "Lord help the mister that comes between me and my sister"?

That's how a family should be, at least so we fantasize. A family is not only a strong bond in reality, but it is an even stronger symbol. The idea of family runs deep into our spiritual and psychic core. It affects us at the emotional as well as the behavioral level. We all want to belong to something larger than ourselves. We want something with which to identify. And our family is our basic unit of identification. That's part of the reason that disturbance in a family, such as child abuse, alcoholism or other pain, creates such pervasive, far-reaching, long-term emotional effects. We idealize the family, what it should be. If our family is not that way, we may feel cheated, hurt, betrayed, even destroyed. The emotional scars may last for years, even a lifetime.

Right now, people are beginning to recognize what they've missed. Many careerists are disillusioned, recognizing that their position, money, cars, houses, and boats haven't bought them the happiness the American dream had promised. Surveys of executives and high achievers show that, more and more, these people are recognizing the need for balance, for more family time. Whereas the family looked like it was dying out a few years ago, now it's on a positive resurgence. The original producers of the TV show "Leave It to Beaver" are receiving increasing numbers of requests for the house plans of the Cleaver house, which was shown during the show's opening credits. It would appear that some people think that if they copy the Cleaver house, they might recapture some of the Cleaver family's loving spirit. People are weary of isolation and disappointment. They are hungering to belong.

What's a "family" anyway? Sociologists would call it a "kinship group." Such a group need not be bound by blood. The "nuclear family" is father, mother, and children. The "extended family" includes one's cousins, aunts, uncles, grandparents, and the rest of the living bloodline. The ancient Hebrews and those of Jesus' day considered one's ancestors to be equally a part of the family, which added a multigenerational, almost eternal aspect to the family concept. We see the same type of identification mentality today in people displaying their family coats of arms or tracing their genealogies. Down deep in the psyche is the notion that I am a better person because of the heroic exploits of my great, great, great, great-grandmother during the Revolutionary War. This is powerful stuff, and no one hoping to motivate others can ignore its fundamental impact.

But kinship does not need to imply blood. Look at the Masons and the Eastern Star, the Kiwanis Club, Lions Club, college fraternities, lodges of all kinds, and the military. All of these organizations succeed because they create a *family* feeling, a bond of loyalty and commitment to common goals. Another "family" is our circle of close friends. For some of us, these people are closer to us than our blood kin. After all, we chose them freely, whereas who our blood relatives are is based on an accident of birth. Hopefully our churches and workplaces also are like a family. Sadly, however, this is usually not the case.

What is it that bonds kinship groups together—especially if bloodline is not involved?

Rituals and symbols are highly important bonding agents.

Formal things like the secret handshake, or the ceremonies at the lodge meeting, to informal routines such as the regular "night out with the boys," or "lunch with the girls," all bond the participants in a powerful way. If you don't think so, just try to change one of these formal or informal rituals or a tradition and hear the hue and cry from the ranks. These simple, outward things become so vitally important because we *identify* with them, and they in turn become part of what defines us as persons. That's why we get so attached to them.

As powerful as these outward signs and symbols are, their motivating power pales in the face of an even greater bonding force—common goals. To be effective motivators, goals cannot be left at the level of vague abstractions. They have to be brought right down to everyday life and breath, and made real to each member of the group. Each member needs to feel a part, as if he or she has a stake in the action and the outcome. Only then will common objectives become a potent motivator. But when that happens, there's no stopping that group! A family feeling will develop that strengthens individual loyalty to the common goal that much more.

As people come together in the service of a common goal, they begin to discover that they have common interests, feelings, and experiences. The things we have in common begin to outweigh our differences. Bonds of mutual loyalty and commitment are strengthened.

But wait a minute! You may be saying, "The employees at my company have common goals. Why aren't we working well together?" They may *know* they have common goals, but to really be effective, employees need to *feel* (1) the goals themselves, (2) the commonness, the mutuality of the goal for the organization as a whole and for each member in particular, (3) that they have a stake in the outcome, and (4) that they will benefit if they help their coworkers succeed.

Most organizations have common goals. They even may have well-drafted mission statements. But often the rest is no more than lip service. The climate in the company may actually work hard to undermine unity at the very moment top management wants to bring teamwork about. Turf wars, power jockeying, contests, sexual harassment, backbiting, and other forms of in-house competition can kill a family feeling very quickly. Sadly, common goals alone do not a family make.

Jesus was keenly aware that if his followers were ever to make an impact on the world, they needed more than just instruction. He could have been content to have his disciples meet him every Sabbath for training, lecture, and discussion. No, this would not cut it.

Jesus' words in this passage summed up his motivational philosophy and practice. His followers weren't just students, interns, functionaries. They were his *family*. Throughout the Gospel accounts, we see the deep feeling of oneness and acceptance Jesus had with his disciples and friends. Jesus loved them in spite of their differences and disputes. He was there through their quarrels and pain. He let them in on the secrets of the Kingdom. He and his disciples lived together and shared their burdens and joys in common. He made them feel not only special, but that they were a special part of him.

It wasn't all sweetness and light. Jesus needed to rebuke his disciples occasionally. He even went so far as to say to hot-headed Peter, "Get thee behind me, Satan." Yet Jesus could say these things without damage to the relationship because the family feeling of love, acceptance, loyalty, and commitment was so strong that, while Peter may have been insulted, he ultimately knew that Jesus meant him no harm. Can our followers feel as secure with our motives when we need to criticize their actions?

Jesus knew the power of the family feeling. He knew what his disciples would face. No less powerful a force could keep them loyal and true under the threat of torture and death, especially after he himself would no longer be with them.

Jesus' disciples and friends were strongly attached to him. Consider the love poured out to him from Mary, Martha, and Lazarus, to name a few. Consider the diverse group of disciples.

Some of them, such as Simon the Zealot and Matthew the tax collector, by rights should have hated each other. Yet Jesus was able to meld them into a functioning family. We can only assume that creating a "family" out of these people was one of his top priorities, and that he had to work at it daily.

What did Jesus do, and what can we do, to create a family loyalty among our followers?

- Show genuine love, concern, and acceptance. Show them that you value them as persons, in spite of their faults. Don't just value them for what they can do for you, but also for who they are. "Unconditional positive regard," as psychologists term it, is so rare in our society, even in our families, that people are hungering for it. If you demonstrate it to your followers, you will most certainly generate their love and loyalty in return.
- Show them the big picture and their role in making the grand dream come true. They need to see what they're aiming for and its importance. They also need to be very clear how vital you consider their particular skills and talents to be in achieving the goal.
- Provide help and emotional support any way you can. Back them up, teach, train, encourage, remind them of their strengths and past successes. When things get rough, people need caring the most.
- Get them thinking "family." Tell them, "We're a family" if it's appropriate to do so in your setting, but only if you're prepared to back it up in action. Use family terms when talking to your team about their work, and about how they should be getting along. Drill family ideals repeatedly into their thinking. This will encourage more rapid, conscious family identification, assuming you're acting accordingly. Some churches instruct their members to refer to each other formally as "brother" or "sister." For example, "I was talking to Brother Smith the other day . . ." This certainly drives the

point home. You don't have to go that far, but making frequent references to your group as a family will help.

• If your group has a special mission or task that sets it apart from other groups or employees, let the group know it. You don't want to encourage feelings of competitiveness or superiority toward other groups, but the specialness of their task is a bonding feature in and of itself. Jesus cultivated this motivation very heavily in his call and training of his disciples. It is a tricky motivator, however. Given our egos, it is very easy for a group to slip into feelings of elitism and competition with other groups. A we-versus-them attitude is destructive. Be on guard for it, and nip it in the bud as soon as you see it developing. Foster an attitude of cooperation with other groups and a joint commitment to the overall goal toward which your group and others might be working.

• Put out brushfires. Jump on disputes between members right away. Don't let feelings fester. Provide outlets for discussion and mechanisms for problem solving, working toward agreed solutions. Don't turn off debate, however. Positive differences of opinion and mild conflict can be very growth-producing and stimulating. These help people stretch their minds. But be prepared to step in if differing opinions become overly emotional and slip into competitive or disruptive behavior.

• Give them inside information. In Matthew 13:10–17 and in Luke 10:23, 24, Jesus explains that the disciples are privy to the secrets of the Kingdom, while the rest of the populace is left guessing. He ends this discourse saying, "Blessed are your eyes for they see, and your ears for they hear." Every family has "secrets," private information that only they should know. From a psychological perspective, it doesn't matter what the private information is! The bonding factor is that "we" have it, "they" don't. Also, knowledge is power. In your particular setting, you may need to be careful with how much and what kind of private information you can express for fear of leakage. Yet you can share with them some of your personal interpretations, discoveries and insights, special techniques, and latest findings that are not yet general knowledge. From a power point of view, two things are important here: that the followers are aware that they are receiving and possess private knowledge, and that you are the source. A careful reading of Luke 10:23, 24 shows that Jesus heavily reinforced these two factors.

- Be yourself, share yourself. In a family, people can feel free to be natural, to be themselves. They can come "home," putting off the image they may have had to put on at work, kicking off their shoes, removing their ties. Within appropriate limits, let your followers see your personal side, your inner feelings. Let them see you behind your role as a leader.

You might even let them see some of your vulnerabilities and let them help you as you are helping them. Good family life is mutual help in action. I can be free not only to give assistance, but also to receive it from my family, whereas outside I might wish to appear more powerful. There is a strong bonding factor in allowing others to help you. It gives them feelings of power and importance in positive ways and reinforces the feeling of equality in the "family."

Jesus also became weak and discouraged on occasion, and his disciples saw it. Perhaps they encouraged him when he was low. Yet Jesus was always the leader. His central role was never compromised. Your role as leader does not have to be compromised even if you need personal help from your followers. There's no disgrace in accepting help. Being leader does not imply omnipotence.

In fact, a leader who is so powerful that he or she needs no personal help from followers actually *discourages* the followers, making them feel less important and useful, and *weakens* the bond between the leader and the team. Down deep, people really don't like omnipotence and perfection. It threatens them. Therefore, they will begin to search out your flaws and capitalize on them with glee. They also need to be needed. Give them the opportunity to help, not only toward the team mission, but toward you personally. It will bond your people and ease your burden.

Building a team is one thing; building a "family" goes much further. But every team needs a family feeling to maximize motivation, loyalty, and output. Nurture this feeling, carefully feed and water it, and watch the power and productivity grow.

9
INDIVIDUALITY

And he sat down opposite the treasury, and watched the
multitude putting money into the [temple] treasury. Many
rich people put in large sums. And a poor widow came,
and put in two copper coins, which make a penny. And he
called his disciples to him, and said to them, "Truly, I say
to you, this poor widow has put in more than all those who
are contributing to the treasury. For they all contributed
out of their abundance; but she out of her poverty has put
in everything she had, her whole living."

Mark 12:41–44

(*Parallel text: Luke 21:1–4*)

Jesus' statement is just a casual observation, a "throwaway"
comment. He wasn't teaching or training. He was just sitting
across the street from the Temple, watching the people. The
widow obviously stood out to Jesus with her poorer clothing,
perhaps mourning attire. So Jesus basically is saying to his
disciples, "Did you notice that . . ." Then Jesus and his disciples moved on. Just a passing comment. Why did two of the
four Gospel chroniclers pick up on it?

Jesus' simple observation is exceedingly profound. "The widow's mite" is one of the most preached-upon texts in all of the Gospels. This is a classic text on stewardship of money, time, and talent. The focus of this preaching is usually the widow and her unselfish love.

But there is another side to this text that is even more important. Jesus' observation about the widow's gift is actually the paradigm for the way he treated others. It reflects a basic principle for understanding, evaluating, and motivating human behavior—the principle of individuality.

Jesus was saying, "Evaluate each person's contribution in terms of the person who made it. See each contribution, skill, or talent in its own context." With one fell swoop, Jesus eliminates comparison as a method of evaluation. This has far-reaching implications for us as leaders, and as friends, parents, and children as well. And it flies in the face of how we normally think of and judge ourselves and others.

Most of us are lax. We take the path of least resistance. It's easier to group people together, assuming they can all perform at the same level. We often feel, "If I can do it, so can they." It's simpler to pick out the "best" one and use it as a yardstick for measuring others. This is what we're really doing when we hold a contest.

Jesus' way takes work. It means getting to know each person's personality: his or her basic capabilities, strengths, talents, limitations. It doesn't mean having a full dossier on each person's background, or analyzing each of your coworkers with the depth of a psychotherapist. Admittedly, that's too herculean a task in most cases. But it does mean taking time to understand the human side of your coworkers, and remembering that when you evaluate or attempt to motivate them, Jesus' way requires more effort, but it yields much higher rewards. People will perform better and be more motivated. They will become more loyal to you. Why?

When you lump people together, some people may feel discounted. They may get the idea that you are not aware of—or don't care about—their particular limitations, or their talents that may be underutilized. They may feel "demotivated."

For a contest to truly work, every contestant must have an equal chance to win. This is so in a lottery, but not in a competition where individual performance is involved. That's because no two people are truly equal in capability and motivation. As a result, contests tend to motivate only those who perceive that they have a good chance to win. Competition *demotivates* those who feel they will probably lose, but those people will never admit it. If you run contests frequently, you probably notice that the same people usually win. How are the rest feeling?

Given our egos, comparison implies that our worth is based on our performance. Comparison breeds competition. When winning becomes the goal, people begin to judge their personal worth, or their capability to do the job, on how well they stack up against others. So if I lose, then I'm not as good as you are.

An art teacher once graded his class by taking the best art project his students created and giving it an A+. Then he used it as the standard by which the rest of the projects were judged. He thought that this would motivate his students to perform. It actually had the opposite effect. The students hated doing the art projects. They became more concerned with how well they'd measure up rather than with how creative or beautiful to make their projects. Worse yet, rather than helping each other, they did their projects in secret, lest another student steal and capitalize upon a good idea. And even worse still, the class began to snub the more artistically talented students, and the talented ones would flaunt their skill and tease the others in return.

Was this typical student behavior? The teacher thought so, but it really wasn't. The teacher himself set up all the backbiting and demotivation by the way he structured his grading system. He (1) created a contest, and (2) did not take individual abilities into account. Why did the students behave so poorly? Because they believed that, in some way, their *personal worth* was on the line. Their egos were involved. They became threatened.

Adults in a performance contest often feel and act the same way. If you don't think so, it's because people don't tell you so. Who in our society is going to admit to feeling threatened by a contest? But the feelings of fear are often there nonetheless.

With this statement to his disciples, Jesus was, in effect, throwing out comparison and competition as a way to motivate others. Jesus knew it didn't work. It has taken us two thousand years and we still don't understand. The latest research on competition and comparison proves Jesus to be correct.[1]

Read the Gospels carefully and you will find that Jesus treated his disciples and others on a very individual basis. He never judged or managed people on a group standard. Every person's worth was assured and never challenged. This did not mean that there were not overall standards of performance toward which all should strive. Rather, Jesus never judged Peter based on John's performance. He knew what each one was capable of producing and handling, and acted accordingly.

Did the "widow's mite" text imply that Jesus saw the widow's minuscule gift to be equal to the generous gifts of the wealthy? Not at all. He actually was saying that her gift was greater given the total sum of her resources. Was Jesus "comparing" her gift to that of the wealthy people? Yes, in the sense that one gift put the others into a relational context. No, in that he was not saying that the wealthy should have given more. Jesus did not condemn anyone in this passage.

What he was saying is that each person's output must be judged on its own merits, given that person's own resources. Don't scoff at the widow's penny because it doesn't match the many shekels donated by the wealthy. Don't look at the gift only on the basis of its outward appearance, but take into account what it means in the context of the ability of the one who gave it.

Jesus knew that we are so impressed with wealth, with excellence, with glitz, with drama, that we tend to overlook or not value enough that which is not as opulent or dazzling. We are so enamored of the big that we discount the small.

Jesus is telling us, "Don't overlook the small, the outwardly insignificant. In its own context, you can see its true worth. Don't let a small contribution be overshadowed by the larger ones. Don't look at just the outcome or the outward appearance. Consider the heart, the motivation of the giver."

How does one boost self-esteem? How does one motivate for peak improvement? How does one reduce destructive comparison and in-group competitiveness, jealousy, and backbiting?

Follow Jesus' principle:

- Treat each one as important in his or her own right.
- Value each one's contributions on its own merits, without comparing it to that of others. People will tend to demotivate themselves by making that comparison on their own. If you catch them doing that, show them that such a comparison is invalid. Each one's contribution, no matter how large or small, is an integral requirement to the success of the overall mission.
- Evaluate each person's contribution based on what was produced, not upon what was lacking. Emphasize what was achieved rather than how the performance may have fallen short of the mark. Again, given human nature, people are usually keenly aware of their own failure. They don't need it rubbed in by us.

In my counseling practice I do quite a bit of work with hypnosis for smoking cessation. On the target quitting date, most people stop smoking entirely. Some, however, still smoke a few cigarettes afterward. Those people usually come into their next visit berating themselves, thinking they've failed. I tell them, "Look how you've succeeded! You used to smoke three packs a day. In the last two days, you've only smoked five cigarettes. Normally you would have smoked 120 cigarettes. Look, you're almost there. Now let's knock out those last little five." Their motivation turns around instantly.

When you focus on how far they've come rather than how far they have to go, they gain a whole new respect for their own power and capability.

- Avoid competition and contests. Rather, help your people to set individual targets when increased motivation is in order, or focus on overall team contribution and each person's vital role in achieving the ultimate goal.
- Show appreciation for each person's uniqueness. This, of course, means taking the time to discover individual talents and potentials.

The widow's mite, with sufficient interest applied, will yield huge dividends.

10
WHAT TO OFFER

"Blessed are the poor in spirit, for theirs is the kingdom of heaven. Blessed are those who mourn, for they shall be comforted. Blessed are the meek, for they shall inherit the earth. Blessed are those who hunger and thirst for righteousness, for they shall be satisfied. Blessed are the merciful, for they shall obtain mercy. Blessed are the pure in heart, for they shall see God. Blessed are the peacemakers, for they shall be called sons of God. Blessed are those who are persecuted for righteousness' sake, for theirs is the kingdom of heaven. Blessed are you when men revile you and persecute you and utter all kinds of evil against you falsely on my account. Rejoice and be glad, for your reward is great in heaven, for so men persecuted the prophets who were before you. You are the salt of the earth; but if salt has lost its taste, how shall its saltness be restored? It is no longer good for anything except to be thrown out and trodden under foot by men. You are the light of the world. A city set on a hill cannot be hid. Nor do men light a lamp and put it under a bushel, but on a stand, and it gives light to all in the house. Let your light so shine before men, that they may see your good works and give glory to your Father who is in heaven."

Matt. 5:3–16

"Therefore I tell you, do not be anxious about your life, what you shall eat or what you shall drink, nor about your body, what you shall put on. Is not life more than food, and the body more than clothing? Look at the birds of the air: they neither sow nor reap nor gather into barns, and yet your heavenly Father feeds them. Are you not of more value than they?"

Matt. 6:25, 26

"Ask, and it will be given you; seek, and you will find; knock, and it will be opened to you. For every one who asks receives, and he who seeks finds, and to him who knocks it will be opened. Or what man of you, if his son asks him for bread, will give him a stone? Or if he asks for a fish, will give him a serpent? If you then, who are evil, know how to give good gifts to your children, how much more will your Father who is in heaven give good things to those who ask him!"

Matt. 7:7–11

(*Parallel texts*: Luke 6:20–23; Luke 12:22–24; Luke 14:34, 35; Luke 11:9–13)

What wonderful words of comfort, of joy, of peace! The first passage quoted above is the Beatitudes (Matt. 5:3–12), which is perhaps the most famous passage of comfort in the whole Bible. Most lovers of Scripture have a special place in their hearts for the Beatitudes, and it is easy to see why. The truth and power of these words have comforted and inspired millions of people in all walks and conditions of life for almost two millennia. Their profound simplicity has never been duplicated nor equaled.

These passages are so poignant, so rich in meaning, that it is very tempting to launch into a content interpretation. Beautiful and sublime in their English translation, these passages have even much more eloquent meaning in the original New Testament Greek. The English loses the vital subtleties of meaning which the original Greek text retains.

But interpretation of content is beyond the scope of this book. Our purpose is a *tactical* interpretation. Not just what Jesus is saying, but more important, *how* he is saying it. What are his methods, and how do those methods help achieve his ultimate purposes? This is the focus of our investigation.

All of the passages quoted are from the Sermon on the Mount, which was possibly not just one sermon delivered on one occasion. Bible scholars are divided about who Jesus' audience actually was.

Some scholars believe that this "sermon" is actually a compilation of Jesus' teaching and preparation which he gave to his inner circle, his disciples, perhaps over the course of several weeks or months. Through Matthew's Gospel, we have a glimpse into Jesus' private training sessions. Therefore, his presentation style is particularly important to us.

The disciples were men called apart for a critical mission (see Chapter 7). They had to be realistically prepared for what lay ahead. They had given up everything to follow Jesus, and follow him they did in spite of poverty, rejection, torture, dungeon, and death. Jesus became discouraged at times. So did the disciples. Jesus needed to motivate these men, to prepare them to carry on in his absence. They were strong individually, but Jesus needed to make them strong in the faith and in their loyalty to God, to Jesus, to each other, and to the people to whom they would preach and provide healing. In short, he had to ready them to act in his stead. No easy task indeed.

Other scholars hold that while the disciples were present, the Sermon on the Mount was actually delivered to a wider audience, perhaps hundreds or even thousands. If this was the case, who would have listened?

The poor, the slaves, the sick, the downtrodden, the workaday folk, the "huddled masses yearning to breathe free" of the oppression of Rome—these would have comprised the bulk of Jesus' audience. Most of Jesus' followers were from the lower strata of the social scale, those who needed hope but had none. People whose lives were often very hard and repetitive, lacking in glamour and the "good things of life." Where do such people go to find peace, joy, satisfaction, comfort?

What could Jesus offer that would transform these people? First of all, he offered hope. Most good leaders hold out hope for success to their followers. Jesus, however, offered hope to the masses in a unique way. He redefined their current experience. How?

As we read the Beatitudes in English, they appear to be a promise of *future* peace: suffer now and you will have your reward in the end. As hopeful as that is, that was not what Jesus was saying.

Jesus was actually speaking in the present tense. Jesus spoke in Aramaic, which was the form of Hebrew spoken in his day. Hebrew and Aramaic have a common exclamation that means "O the blessedness of . . ." This is the form that Jesus used when he first uttered the Beatitudes: "Oh the blessedness of the poor in spirit."[1] This is not a casual statement, but rather almost a shout of joy.

Each of the Beatitudes follows the same format. Jesus was not saying, "You will be blessed," but "In your pain and suffering you're blessed right now, right here, today!" The tone of the original language is one of congratulation. The blessedness into which the people had already entered is reason for joy and celebration. According to William Barclay, "The very form of the beatitudes is a statement of the joyous thrill and the radiant gladness of the Christian life."[2]

People's life was hard. Jesus in effect called it joyous. It was as if he were saying, "Look into the current moment, your current situation, and see the other side of it, what's behind it. You have the blessing right now through your sorrow. When everything's running smoothly, you don't grow much. Through mourning, struggling, and persecution, you really experience blessing and depth of growth. Praise your current pain, for you are better and stronger for it."

Jesus was telling the disciples and the others how fortunate they were to be in their current state. That is powerful motivation indeed, when people come to redefine negatives in positive terms. Furthermore, in the Beatitudes, Jesus was pointing out the benefits they were then receiving and would receive in the future.

This may sound like an insignificant grammatical issue, but it is not. It is one thing to hold out the carrot, promising a reward in the future. It is quite another to help people see that they were beginning to experience their reward and their benefits then and there. In the carrot approach, the reward is an abstraction, a promise out there that really may or may not come to pass. However, when those in the audience were able to redefine their current experience in positive terms, the rewards became real, and that helped keep them going.

Was Jesus conning his listeners? No way. Jesus never promised that which was untrue or which he couldn't deliver. It's a con game when you commit to something for your followers that really you can't deliver, or which won't come to pass. They see through that scam and will no longer trust you.

When Jesus redefined his listeners' current situation as blessedness, he knew well the spiritual principles that were operating. Thus his pronouncements were all sound and ultimately verifiable in terms of God's promises and human experience.

Jesus also offered a realistic portrayal of which privations the disciples and others who followed him would face (Matt. 5:12; see also Chapter 11 in this book). While no one enjoys being told he will suffer, it is encouraging to know the truth. Then one can adequately prepare and will not be disillusioned when the troubles come. Those who suspect they are dying of cancer generally prefer to be told flat out what their chances are rather than having the doctors and relatives beat around the bush and promise recovery when there is little hope to survive.

The disciples and his other followers were no different. Following Jesus would prove fatal for many of them. They had a right to know. But in the very next breath Jesus reiterated their blessedness, and did one thing more. He made their suffering noble and holy by likening his followers to the chosen prophets of God who preceded them and whom they honored and respected. He linked his followers and the prophets together, reinforcing the specialness of the role that the disciples and other followers held. They would not suffer in vain, but they would be heroes, doing their duty in the service of God.

Down through the centuries the Christian martyrs considered it an honor to suffer and die for their Lord. People have felt the same way about other causes, core beliefs, and principles, and about their nations. For many soldiers, there is glory in dying in battle, and in our nation we have a strong tradition of according extra honor and hero status to our war dead. Jesus was well aware of this motivation. He spoke on several occasions in the Gospels as to the suffering the loyal would face.

Jesus predicted tribulation, but with it he offered glory, a great reward in heaven. Also, prepared people may find the actual trials to be not as hard as they had imagined. And by being prepared in advance, they can develop specific coping skills. To be blindsided by tragedy, to get hit with tribulation after being lulled into complacency, especially when you could have been told the truth in advance, is particularly disheartening and can quickly destroy belief in a leader's credibility.

In Matthew 5:13–16, Jesus reiterated in glowing metaphors the central value the believers possessed. At the same time, he reminded them of the tremendous responsibility that their key role carried with it. Almost always in Jesus' discourses, one's special importance was counterbalanced by one's duties.

Having a vital role is a key motivator. Having vital responsibilities makes the role even more important and worthwhile. So Jesus' exhortations were actually increasing his adherents' morale and loyalty. It boosted their self-esteem. You give great responsibility only to those who can handle it. Therefore, people feel complimented when they are offered important tasks.

Encouraged, positive-thinking people see important responsibilities as opportunities for growth and development as well as for honor. They feel challenged, and will rise to the challenge as best they can.

Of course, they must perceive that successful fulfillment of the responsibility lies within their grasp. Jesus never doubted for a minute that his disciples and other followers could fulfill their missions, and he communicated that confidence to them by *assuming* their capability. They were exhorted to behave in ways befitting their role. Their success was always defined in terms of whether or not they did as they were told; never was there a question as to whether or not they were *capable* of following through. If their leader has full confidence in the troops, the troops are much more likely to have confidence in themselves. After all, so the notion goes, the leader ought to know best.

Jesus also offered comfort. In essence, he told the people that if they stayed on the right track, their needs would be met. The passage in Matthew 6, quoted at the beginning of the chapter, ends this way: "But seek first his kingdom and his righteousness, and all these things (food, clothing, life's necessities) shall be yours as well" (Matt. 6:33).

Jesus' audience had a right to be worried about food and clothing. It was rare for the average person to have more than one or two tunics, and for the poor, homeless, and sick, there was constant uncertainty as to when they would see food again. Jesus faces these pressing needs with "Don't be anxious about your life, what you shall eat or what you shall drink, or about your body, what you shall put on." Why not? God will meet their need. But Jesus indicated that the people also have a responsibility to seek first the kingdom and God's righteousness, to live a holy life.

These words, like the Beatitudes, are tremendous words of comfort. Jesus zeroed right in to his listeners' most pressing needs and promised they would be met. Talk about selling the benefits! He told them to stop struggling, that they would be taken care of. Their prayers will be answered, if only they ask. They will find what they need, provided they seek. This is not struggle, clawing out of fear, but the responsibility to act on one's faith. Jesus is not saying, "Sit back, and God will dump all his riches in your lap." Again, we have a responsibility to do our part. If we do, we shall have our reward.

Finally, Jesus offered *action*. Throughout the Gospels, Jesus took action to back up his words. He healed the sick and the lame, made the blind to see, fed the five thousand and four thousand and even raised Lazarus from the dead. I have not included verses citing Jesus' action at the outset of this chapter, because the other chapters provide sufficient examples.

Returning to the twentieth century, the needs that we face in uplifting and motivating our followers may not be anywhere near as dramatic. Our followers' lives may not be in danger, but their careers may be on the line. In most cases they are not likely to be poor, oppressed, or starving, although some of your followers may face these privations.

Yet we all must battle fear, hesitancy, doubt, low self-esteem—in ourselves and in our followers. Thus Jesus' words and his style are very relevant for us as leaders. We have to motivate our followers, help them over the rough spots.

As we read the passages from the Sermon on the Mount, we can substitute our own words to relate to our people's needs. Jesus' technique was just as powerful as the words he used. Let's briefly summarize how he motivated his audience.

• He gave them hope, not by promising vague future outcomes, but by redefining their current situations in positive terms. He showed them how they were actually blessed and benefiting through their current difficulties.

   What difficulties or problems entangle your people? Try redefining them in positive terms. Think it through, write it down. Run the positive ramifications through in your mind. Only when you come to believe it in your heart and soul are you ready to explain it to your followers.

- He spelled out a realistic appraisal of the problems his followers would face. He didn't pussyfoot, minimize, or gloss over difficulties. He helped prepare them and offered a challenge for heroism and glory, identifying the faithful with the prophets of old.

  What opportunities for recognition and heroism does your situation present? With what heroes can you link your people? What risks will your people face? Challenges excite people, yet risks can also threaten them.

- Jesus showed confidence that his people would be able to face the challenges head-on and succeed. He never doubted their capability; he was there to help them become stronger and more capable.

  What can you do to demonstrate confidence in your followers, to excite them to take the necessary risks, build their confidence, and allay their fear? Notice that Jesus never tried to quell fear by saying, "It won't be so bad." Rather, he reinforced people's inner power and the fact that God was on their side.

- Jesus linked together people's value and their responsibilities. At the same time he complimented them, he reinforced what they needed to be doing. He spelled these duties out as a challenge, a level of performance for which to strive.

- He offered comfort. Comfort through words, reminding them of their special place in God's kingdom and of their power. Comfort through the relationship his followers had with him, that he was there for them.

  Do your people need words of comfort? Perhaps they do, more than you know. There's comfort not only in your words, but in the fact that they are a team, they face the foes together, and in knowing that you're there for them, to help them along.

- Jesus offered action. He backed them up, he assisted, he empowered.

  What actions can you take to back up your words, to make your presence powerful and real?

11
COURAGE UNDER FIRE

"And when they bring you before the synagogues and the rulers and the authorities, do not be anxious how or what you are to answer or what you are to say; for the Holy Spirit will teach you in that very hour what you ought to say."

Luke 12:11, 12

"But the Counselor, the Holy Spirit, whom the Father will send in my name, he will teach you all things, and bring to your remembrance all that I have said to you."

John 14:21

(*Parallel texts:* Matt. 24:9–14; Mark 13:9–13; Luke 21:12–19)

"When they arrest you, don't be scared. God will speak through you," Jesus is saying. Is Jesus being unrealistic? The death sentence in Jesus' day was often carried out in the most grizzly, torturous ways, to the satisfaction of bloodthirsty onlookers. If your very life is in danger, you know you're supposed to have faith, but aren't you going to be at least a bit worried?

Jesus himself was cool and in complete control before Pilate and Herod, knowing that he was assuredly going to be crucified. Jesus was, however, the Son of God. We could expect calmness under fire from him, but how can he really expect the same of us? Yet Jesus says, "Don't be afraid."

Good advice, but how can it really work?

Jesus is saying to rely on the principle of faith. We're not talking about "belief" here, in the sense of assenting to certain ideas. This is passive. In this sense of "faith," I could say that I believe in God, that the Bible is His word, that the Ten Commandments were given to Moses, and so forth.

Rather, Jesus means to rely on God, to trust Him. The theologian Kierkegaard spoke of a leap of faith, likening it to jumping off a cliff, knowing that God will keep you from harm. Have you ever literally tried that? Neither have I. But Kierkegaard would assert that nothing less is real faith.

How does it work? If I get myself in a jam, God isn't going to reach out of Heaven and snatch me away to a safe place. No, I'll have to face the music and see it through to the end. I may have to cope with it all alone.

But am I really alone? No! God is with me, and I have to trust that His will, not mine, be done. Jesus has promised us that if God be with us, no one can prevail against us.

We are a channel for the Holy Spirit to work through us. If the channel is open, we and those whose lives we touch can experience God's power. But we can also block the channel. Then nothing can get through either way. When this happens, we are still in the palm of God's hand, but we can't experience that reality because our head is in a different place.

Now, we can't be aware and self-aware at the same time. The mind can only focus on one thing at a time. To be "aware" means to be in full touch with our environment, with what's going on. It's being in the moment, able to respond in a give-and-take way to the circumstances as they unfold. To be self-aware means to be lost in our own thoughts, absorbed in contemplation, to be concerned with the past or the future instead of the now, to be wondering, thinking, evaluating, worrying. Self-awareness shuts down awareness, slows our reaction time, blocks our sensitivity to our environment. Most of all, it blocks the channel to our own creative subconscious mind and to God.

A simple example of awareness versus self-awareness is what happens when you drive your car. You start the engine and take off. Your mind is on your driving as you stop at red lights and pass through intersections. Then you get onto the expressway. Your mind shifts. You start thinking about that important meeting you have this morning. You rehearse what you'll say, you anticipate the possible outcome. You have shifted at that instant into self-awareness. You get to work, but "you don't know how you got there," and you lost track of time. If someone had asked you about something on the side of the road while you were contemplating the meeting, you probably couldn't have told the person about it, because you didn't "see" it. Your eyes may have physically seen it—after all, they were working well enough to get you to work safely—but it didn't register in your conscious mind.

Worry is the most potent form of self-awareness, and also the biggest block to the channel. You can't be anxious and creative at the same time. You can't be worrying and open to the Spirit's leading. It just doesn't work. When you're anxious, you're struggling. You're trying to sort things out. Your mind is constricted. It's hung up on the object of your fear, or on fear itself. You cannot struggle and trust at the same time. Trust requires, and produces, calmness and peace. It is physically impossible, however, given the nature of the human nervous system, to be tense and relaxed at the same time.

With training and consistent practice in meditation, prayer, relaxation, self-hypnosis, and related methods, one can learn to relax so well that when one becomes upset, the relaxation takes over and calms the fear, reducing the tension and producing inner peace. This is a complex biochemical process which takes place in the human body. Such relaxation methods have been shown to reduce stress, speed healing, and lengthen people's lives.

More important for our purposes, relaxation promotes the flow of ideas, either from the leading of the Holy Spirit, or from our own creative subconscious. When was the last time you had a good idea when you were tense or nervous? I'll bet you groped for ideas like a drowning sailor struggles to reach a life preserver, but you didn't get any useful thoughts. Later, when you calmed down, the ideas you needed came to mind freely and easily.

Here's how it works. Your subconscious mind is the seat of your creativity, and also is the central file for all your past knowledge, learning, wisdom, and experience. It contains megatimes more information and ideas than you are consciously able to recall or express at any given time. Your subconscious mind also knows what you need, and it will supply that need, provided you are relaxed and unbothered. Fear, on the other hand, gets your adrenaline flowing and prepares you in other physical ways for flight or fight. By so doing, it shuts down the channel to the creative side of your subconscious. Instinctual feelings and actions take over, and your mind shifts into worry gear. Unfortunately, mentally you end up spinning your wheels and getting nowhere. It's like revving the engine of your car when you're on a muddy dirt road. When the mud stops flying, you know where you will still be. Rather, the solution is to press the gas pedal slowly and evenly. Take it calm and relaxed. Travel an inch at a time. Only then will you have any hope of getting free of the mud.

So here's the fundamental principle: cool's the rule, hot gets shot. Jesus knew it. He knew that in the time of crisis, your only hope is to relax, get out of your own way, and let God use your creative subconscious to give you the words and ideas you need to solve the problem.

This principle works in every setting. As a competition coach, I've found that the only way for athletes to do their best in the heat of competition is to be mentally relaxed during play. Only then can they reach their peak performance state. Only then can they be sure that their nervousness won't destroy their performance.

Likewise, on the public platform, I've found that when I'm nervous, the words and ideas don't flow. When I take my mind off myself and my performance, however, I can loosen up, and I get fantastic ideas during the course of the speech that I had never even considered before I ascended the platform. I'm sure you've noticed the same thing in your experiences.

Trust God.

Trust yourself.

How?

Trust takes time to build. Trust and faith will ultimately cancel fear, but in the beginning, fear is more powerful.

Therefore, trust must be nurtured. There are a number of ways you can develop the trust that leads to calmness and courage under fire.

- Develop your zeal for your mission. If you have a passion for your plans and point of view, you will automatically have more courage. Zeal works wonders in quickly building trust in yourself. A zealous person is ready to go from the gut, act on instinct. She's into it before she stops to worry. It's like getting into Heaven a half hour before the devil knows you're dead!
- Build your knowledge. Knowledge in your subject area is power. It breeds confidence. The more you know about a given subject, the better able you'll be to field questions and to frame responses. The more you'll be able to trust in yourself when the chips are down. Your creative subconscious will have that much bigger a reservoir to tap.
- Mentally rehearse. If you expect to have to defend your position or get yourself out of a particular predicament, just close your eyes and visualize yourself handling this situation. Trust your creative subconscious to come up with ideas.

Practice different solutions in your mind. Tell yourself positive affirmations: that you will succeed, that just the right words and actions will come to mind just as you need them, and so on. Program your mind for success. The more often you do this in a relaxed state, the more confidence you will have and the more likely you will be to click automatically into the solution you've rehearsed when you have to face the situation for real.

- Practice. If you have to give a defense, make a presentation or a speech, or handle a difficult situation, practice. Role-play if necessary. Again, when you have to do it for real, you don't always have time to think. Good practice gives you confidence and a patterned set of behaviors which you can implement automatically, without having to think. Why do you think military paratroopers practice parachute jumping so much at home before they have to do it in conflict? Practice not only builds confidence, it also creates automatic responses.

   Faith does not mean winging it. Sometimes circumstances happen so suddenly that you don't have time to prepare. But to wing it when the stakes are high and preparation time is ample is foolhardy. God would want and expect you to give yourself every advantage you can.

- Practice relaxing. Use meditation, prayer, self-hypnosis, centering, or other ways to relax. It is beyond our scope to describe these here. Numerous books and articles have been written on each of these techniques.

- Most important, pray. Ask for guidance. Ask God to protect and assist you. Do your part, and then settle back, open the channel, and allow God to do his, trusting two basic truths:

God's will will be done, and
You can do all things through Christ, who strengthens you.

12
MAXIMIZING THE IMPACT OF YOUR MESSAGE

And behold, a lawyer stood up to put him to the test, saying, "Teacher, what shall I do to inherit eternal life?" He said to him, "What is written in the law? How do you read?" And he answered, "You shall love the Lord your God with all your heart, and with all your soul, and with all your strength, and with all your mind; and your neighbor as yourself." And he said to him, "You have answered right; do this, and you will live." But he, desiring to justify himself, said to Jesus, "And who is my neighbor?" Jesus replied, "A man was going down from Jerusalem to Jericho, and he fell among robbers, who stripped him and beat him, and departed, leaving him half dead. Now by chance a priest was going down that road; and when he saw him he passed by on the other side. So likewise a Levite, when he came to the place and saw him, passed by on the other side. But a Samaritan, as he journeyed, came to where he was; and when he saw him, he had compassion, and went to him and bound up his wounds, pouring on oil and wine; then he set him on his own beast and brought him to an inn, and took care of him. And the next day he took out

> two denarii and gave them to the innkeeper, saying, 'Take
> care of him; and whatever more you spend, I will repay
> you when I come back.' Which of these three, do you think,
> proved neighbor to the man who fell among the robbers?"
> He said, "The one who showed mercy on him." And Jesus
> said to him, "Go and do likewise."
>
> Luke 10:25–37
>
> (*Parallel texts* to Luke 10:25–28: Matt. 22:35–40;
> Mark 12:28–31)

What do you remember? Think back to the past classes or
training workshops you attended. What do you recall from the
last great motivational speaker you heard? Was it the outline or
theoretical content? Not likely. You recall the stories.

Jesus wasn't a lecturer, he was a storyteller. He was asked
many questions and he preached countless sermons. He could
have answered with a definition or given a theoretical explanation. Rather, he took more time and told a story to make his
point. Why?

Myths, parables, metaphors, allegories—these are all ways to
get a point across by describing or portraying it in terms of
something else everyone understands: an analogy, which may
be either fictional or factual. Here's another example:

> At that time the disciples came to Jesus, saying, "Who is
> the greatest in the kingdom of heaven?" And calling to him
> a child, he put him in the midst of them, and said, "Truly,
> I say to you, unless you turn and become like children, you
> will never enter the kingdom of heaven. Whoever humbles
> himself like this child, he is the greatest in the kingdom of
> heaven."
>
> Matt. 18:1–4

From the dawn of history, shamans and prophets have relied
on the power of story and metaphor to influence human experience. In every society, the ritual storytellers have been accorded high honor. Even today in America this is often so, with

the most famous receiving up to fifty thousand dollars per appearance.

Parable power. In an age when many people think of stories as kid stuff, the intuitive leader taps into this treasure trove of influence, sprinkling the salt and pepper of stories and metaphors liberally into the meat and potatoes of his or her daily discourse.

Why do stories and metaphors have such effect? For the sake of simplicity, I will use the term *story* to refer to both teaching stories and brief analogies.

- Stories capture human experience. They tap into the common feelings and reactions that we all share. We can weep with the victim, root for the underdog, cheer for the hero. They enable us to empathize, which helps us not only to hear but to "own" the point being made.
- Stories plumb the depth of feeling. Reason rides the horse of emotion. People don't take action on the basis of reason alone. Passion is what motivates. Properly constructed stories arouse passion, feeling. They help us not only understand the point, but also feel it. The context reaches our heads, the stories touch our hearts.
- Stories provide examples of preferred behavior. Heroes and heroines serve as models. We hear how they got out of scrapes or masterfully executed a plan. The implication, when we hear such tales, is "go and do likewise," or be careful to avoid their mistakes.
- Stories provide an object of identification. Taking this fact one step further, what happens when we identify with a particular character? We find ourselves behaving like that character automatically. Usually the identification process operates at the subconscious level. When we admire someone and begin to identify with him or her, it's as if our actions went on autopilot. Once I was a counselor at a summer camp. I strongly admired the camp director. Before too long, I found myself speaking like him. I picked up his accent and man-

nerisms. Because of the subconscious nature of identification, it is an extremely potent phenomenon, which every leader should nurture. Not only are behaviors incorporated, so are attitudes and values.

- Properly crafted stories link us to our heritage, our traditions. They remind us of our roots and our cultural, racial, ethnic, or corporate identity. Thus, they bond us to others of our kind, fostering stronger group identification and pride.

- Finally, stories do all of the above in an enjoyable way. We all want to be entertained, while few of us enjoy being lectured. When we're being entertained by a fascinating tale, we often hang on every word, and the message slips in almost subliminally. Our defenses are down and we're more reachable and teachable in those precious powerful moments.

As a leader, then, work to develop your storytelling technique. You can do it. Don't think that you have to be personality-plus or a natural entertainer or comedian in order to be effective at telling tales. In fact, the power of your position as leader may assist you by adding authority to your stories, sometimes making them more believable or important in the minds of your listeners because you, the leader, told the story.

How to Tell a Teaching Story with Impact

Here are several tips that will help you develop your skills in this area.

- Visualize yourself as a storyteller. You are, although many people think that this is a talent possessed by only a few. If you ever told a personal experience to someone else, or told a joke, you're a storyteller! Being a good storyteller takes practice, but you can learn how.

- Practice looking for analogies, metaphors, and images. A teaching story is just an expanded analogy. If you read through the Gospels, you frequently encounter Jesus saying,

"The Kingdom of Heaven is like . . ." That's the formula: something you want to discuss or get across "is like" something else that we basically understand.

Once you start looking for analogies, symbols, or images for everyday situations or experiences, you will begin to *think* in analogies. When that happens, you've got it made. Metaphors will quickly come to mind when you need them, and you can drop them in spontaneously to spice up impromptu conversation.

- Practice expanding your analogies. An analogy, metaphor, or teaching story is symbolic. Once you've shifted your conversation into that frame of reference, you can play with it and elaborate on it, staying with that symbol to make further points. Here's an example: The large corporation is like a giant naval flotilla—many ships sailing in formation. Different kinds of ships with different purposes are linked together with a common purpose and destination. The CEO is the admiral, stationed on the bridge of the command ship, giving orders to and receiving information from the captains of the other ships (departments) under his command.

  Think how you can expand the flotilla metaphor to discuss competition and cooperation, singleness of purpose, or communication breakdowns. Here's another aspect: the guys in the engine room make the ship go, but they cannot see where their ship is headed. They rely on orders from the bridge. Can you use that analogy to describe duty, obligation, dependence, or other power or human resource issues in your organization?

- *KISS* (Keep It Short and Simple). Unless you're sitting out in the woods by a campfire telling ghost stories, you don't want to make your stories long or involved. Short and to the point— that's the key to a teaching story. Remember that the story is not an end in itself. It is only an illustration to help make your point clearer. The more complex the story is, the more it can confuse your listener and detract from your main point. If you read Jesus' parables, you will notice that they rarely occupy more than a few verses.

- Develop a vocabulary of power and feeling words, and use them in your stories. Many of us, especially males, have a difficult time describing emotion or talking about how someone else must have felt in a given situation. Part of that difficulty is a lack of a sufficiently full vocabulary to express emotion. The more words you know that express broader ranges of feelings, the easier it will be to move your listeners to empathy and emotional involvement when you describe a hero's or heroine's reaction in a story.

  The degree of our vocabulary about a given subject also reflects that subject's importance to us. The Arabs have over fifty words to describe "camel." How many English words can you think of for that beast? Camels just aren't that important to most of us. Make people's feelings and emotional reactions important to you, and you will be more convincing when you involve emotion in your stories and appeals for action.

- Be sure that your story or metaphor taps either a universal experience to which anyone can relate, or something that your audience intimately knows. Don't use complex engineering examples with an audience of social workers. They probably won't understand, and your story will not only lack impact, it may actually provide more confusion than clarity to your point.

  The students in one of our area high schools recently put on Thornton Wilder's play *By the Skin of Our Teeth*. It is an allegory dealing with issues of survival, and the human spirit. The play was written in 1943, when the outcome of World War II was very much up for grabs. Playgoers who witnessed the original production may well have gone home to blackout curtains and air raid drills. The students did a credible job of performing, but the actors and most of the audience had no concept of the true impact of the play since they were all born and have lived in a world of relative peace. No matter how good the story is, if your listeners can't relate to it, it's the wrong story.

- Don't preach or moralize. This turns people off and may cast you in a position of being seen as holier than thou. If your story has a moral, let that moral stand on its own and sink in. However, a simple wrap-up statement is useful. A one-sentence wrap-up (as in the ending of the preceding paragraph) ties the story back to reality and to the main point. A question could do the same, as in the parable of the Good Samaritan, which opened this chapter.

- Don't overinterpret the story to your audience or expound on the main point. People will respond to symbols and allegories in very private, personal ways, often taking more from your story than you intended to give. They will see aspects of the story that are personally relevant to themselves.

- Don't overdo it. As too much salt can ruin the taste of a meal, too many stories and metaphors can turn people off. Use them carefully and judiciously, saving them for backing up your most important points.

You don't need to save stories and metaphors for formal speeches. They work very well with informal groups at meetings, around the table at lunch, and one to one.

Where to Find Stories and Analogies

The world is full of stories. If you begin to look for them, you'll find more than you can ever use. Here are some sources to consider:

- The Bible, the Talmud—Bible stories and tales from religious tradition often reflect very basic human situations and can be inspirational and instructive from a completely secular perspective.
- Fairy tales, Aesop's *Fables*, Rudyard Kipling's *Just So* stories, other children's classics such as *The Little Engine That Could*,

Alice in Wonderland. Very brief vignettes or the whole short story from children's literature can not only make a point but also recapture the child in us, entertaining us as we listen and learn.

- Movies, especially the Disney classics that have become part of our cultural lore, and current popular ones that many of your audience would have seen.

- Borrow tales from other speakers. Never steal; always give credit to your source.

- Excerpts from novels, especially classics or popular ones.

- Current events and relevant news items.

- Your organization—every organization is a treasure trove of tips and tales. Check with your company "historian." Every organization has one—someone who knows the history of the firm inside and out. When talking about the people in your organization, always be positive, but don't exaggerate. You don't want to embarrass anyone. Also be careful not to set up as heroes or heroines those people whom the rank and file do not respect.

- *Yourself*—your own experiences perhaps make the best stories of all. By self-disclosing, you show your courage and your humanity. Personal experiences may also be the most powerful tales because you actually lived them, and can bring to them all the relevant feeling and action.

Remember that, as a leader, you are always "onstage." You have the opportunity and power to influence with what you say in every situation in which you find yourself. The higher up you are in the organization, the broader your sphere of influence is and the more powerful your words become. That's a fact of life. Remembering this and capitalizing on it appropriately in each situation, even in your everyday speaking, will add immeasurably to your impact.

13
SHOW AND TELL

"And when you pray, you must not be like the hypocrites; for they love to stand and pray in the synagogues and at the street corners, that they may be seen by men. Truly, I say to you, they have their reward. But when you pray, go into your room and shut the door and pray to your Father who is in secret; and your Father who sees in secret will reward you. And in praying do not heap up empty phrases as the Gentiles do, for they think that they will be heard for their many words. Do not be like them, for your Father knows what you need before you ask him. Pray then like this:

> Our Father who art in heaven,
> Hallowed be thy name.
> Thy kingdom come,
> Thy will be done,
> On earth as it is in heaven.
> Give us this day our daily bread;
> And forgive us our debts,
> As we also have forgiven our debtors;

And lead us not into temptation,
but deliver us from evil."

Matt. 6:5–13

(*Parallel texts*: Mark 11:25, 26; Luke 11:2–4)

And he called to him his twelve disciples and gave them authority over unclean spirits, to cast them out, and to heal every disease and every infirmity. . . . These twelve Jesus sent out [two by two—Mark 6:7], charging them, "Go nowhere among the Gentiles, and enter no town of the Samaritans, but go rather to the lost sheep of the house of Israel. And preach as you go, saying, 'The kingdom of heaven is at hand.' Heal the sick, raise the dead, cleanse lepers, cast out demons. You received without pay, give without pay. Take no gold, nor silver, nor copper in your belts, no bag for your journey, nor two tunics, nor sandals, nor a staff; for the laborer deserves his food. And whatever town or village you enter, find out who is worthy in it, and stay with him until you depart. As you enter the house, salute it. And if the house is worthy, let your peace come upon it; but if it is not worthy, let your peace return to you. And if any one will not receive you or listen to your words, shake off the dust from your feet as you leave that house or town. Truly, I say to you, it shall be more tolerable on the day of judgment for the land of Sodom and Gomorrah than for that town."

Matt. 10:1, 5–16

(*Parallel texts*: Mark 6:7–11; Luke 9:1; Luke 10:1–11)

How do you get your desires across to your followers in such a way that they will carry them out in the proper manner?

This is the critical problem of delegation and giving instructions. Ultimately the effective leader must duplicate herself if she is to cover a broader scope or maximize her impact. This means engaging the assistance of others. Getting the job done right is a thorny problem, and books have been written on it. This short chapter is not meant to be exhaustive on this issue, but highlights two examples of how Jesus coped with the problem.

The first selection is the Lord's Prayer from the Sermon on the Mount. With the religious Jews of Jesus' day, how one addressed God was quite ritualized. Quite often, the rabbis would state prayers for their followers to say. Jesus was doing the same, and making personal prayer quite simple. Perhaps he was cutting through some of the ritual, saying in essence, "Let's get to the heart of the matter."

Our purpose in this chapter is not to discuss Jesus the rabbi, but Jesus the trainer.

Jesus was concerned not just with what people did when they prayed; he went a step further. He started not with the specific how-tos, but he addresses the underlying attitude the people ought to have. "Before doing anything, do it for the right reasons," Jesus is saying, "and do it in the right manner." Thus, Jesus, in training his listeners in a new method, addressed both the head and the heart.

How often do we train people to do a specific thing and neglect addressing the manner and attitude in which it is to be carried out? We so often leave that to chance, sometimes with tragic results.

Sometimes the Thomas Beckett syndrome occurs. King Henry II of England appointed his best friend and supporter, Thomas Beckett, as Archbishop of Canterbury. Once he was elevated, however, Beckett began to oppose Henry on significant issues. One night Henry was drinking with several of his barons and commented in a drunken state, "I wish someone would rid me of that pesky priest." Upon hearing Henry's words, the barons, who hated Beckett, went straightaway to Canterbury and slew Thomas Beckett while he was saying Mass. Henry never wanted Beckett to die, and bitterly mourned his passing.

The point is that when you give casual instructions, or just deal with the specifics, you may leave to chance *how* the instructions will be carried out. If you don't tell your people, they will follow the instructions in the manner in which *they* wish, which in some situations may cause problems.

Jesus was concerned here not just with the letter of the law, but with the spirit of it as well. For it is the attitude that gives true meaning to the action.

Once he made clear how one should go about praying, Jesus then presented a model prayer that could be used by rote, as is. In other words, rather than just telling them how to say it, he wrote the script. How much more simple could he have made it? His prayer addressed the main aspects of life in a simple but profound way. Now anyone could pray properly to the Father.

How to carry out a mission is a much more complex matter, and here again Jesus demonstrated a superb tactical approach. Let's examine it step by step.

The original Greek text speaks of Jesus "charging" the disciples in terms suggesting how a general would command his troops. Jesus made it clear from the outset that what he was telling them to do was serious business. These were their marching orders, and they were to follow through. The original text conveys a sense of importance in Jesus' tone and the assertion of his supreme authority as leader which is inadequately rendered in the English translation.

Next Jesus gave the disciples power over unclean spirits and to heal diseases. Somehow the disciples appear to have been granted supernatural abilities. For our purposes, what Jesus did was to fully fit his troops for the task they were to fulfill. This is a critical step which many leaders overlook. Jesus gave them not only a reasonable task but also the authority necessary to carry it out.

How often have you been given an assignment but lacked sufficient authority to back it up? Responsibility without authority is deadening. It kills morale because it places the delegates in an awkward position, like having to fight in the boxing ring with one hand tied behind your back. You have to interface with new people or initiate a new plan, but you can't carry it through to completion. It makes you look less competent or knowledgeable in the eyes of your observers.

The far greater insult of responsibility without authority is the lack of trust it implies. It suggests that you're capable of getting the ball rolling—that you're okay as a functionary—but that you're not creative, wise, informed, or smart enough to manage on your own.

Jesus' disciples were ordinary men. Yet he was able to entrust them with extraordinary assignments and opportunity because he did a thorough job of training, preparing, and empowering them. When he sent them out, therefore, he could rest easy, trusting that they would be successful. If we observe the flow of the entire Gospel context, we can deduce that Jesus did not send them out prematurely, but only after they were properly readied. Jesus apparently knew the timing and pacing of the tasks of his ministry and followed his "schedule."

Jesus sent them out two by two. It would have been characteristic of Jesus to pair his disciples carefully for this mission so that each individual's skills would complement those of the other man in the dyad. Jesus knew that their task would be tough. In fact, in Matthew 10:16 and the verses following, which were not quoted at the outset of this chapter, Jesus warns the disciples of what difficulties they might face.

Pairing the disciples served several purposes. First, it provided moral and emotional support. Each had a partner with whom he could share the task, along with its joys and discouragements. Next, it broadened the skill base and effectiveness of the team, as often two heads are five times better than one. Also, it reduced egomania. Because two people were involved, no one person could hog the glory.

Jesus charged the disciples not to go into heavily Gentile-populated regions nor into Samaria. This effectively limited the disciples to the area of Galilee. There were several reasons for this. From a theological perspective, Jesus' message was to be given "to the Jews first, and then to the Greeks." God's chosen people were to have the primary opportunity of accepting him.

Although they were of Hebrew background, the Samaritans were considered ritually unclean by devout Jews, and Jews were forbidden to do business, socialize, or even converse with Samaritans. Galilee, however, was an area of political unrest, one that would be more liberal-thinking and more open to new ideas.

From a tactical point of view, Jesus limited his objectives, and therefore concentrated his "firepower." Had he expanded the terrain that his disciples could cover, he would have spread his resources too thin. Also, the disciples were Jews with little apparent exposure to other cultures. Thus they would have been unprepared to minister to the Gentile mind-set, which at that time and place would have been heavily influenced by Greek philosophy and thought (see the Afterword for more background information). Jews and Greeks thought very differently. For example, to the Greek, "wisdom" was logic and reason, whereas to the Jew, "wisdom" was the knowledge of God. It would take someone as educated and worldly-wise as the Apostle Paul to properly relate to the Gentiles.

To go to the Samaritans would invite rejection. After all, to the Jews, the Samaritans were less than dogs, and the feeling was mutual. It would have been like an Israeli today trying to achieve credibility and an unbiased acceptance from the PLO! No, Jesus concentrated his men in the region where they would have the greatest probability of a positive response.

Next, Jesus spelled out the ground rules for his disciples' activities and conduct. Jesus gave very specific rules—for what to say, where to stay and for how long, what to do while they were in a particular town, and even how to pack for the journey. He also told them what to say and do if they were rejected.

In so doing, Jesus set specific parameters. But within those bounds, the disciples were free to exercise their authority and structure their preaching and activities as they saw fit. I can picture Peter and John sitting before a campfire on the eve of entering a new town, planning what each was going to say and mapping out their strategy.

If you closely examine Jesus' instructions, the disciples really had quite a bit of latitude. Jesus held them accountable for the types of activities to be carried out, but *how* they were to go about it—the process—was largely left up to the disciples. They had great opportunity for creativity and independence within the basic framework Jesus set.

The disciples operated in Jesus' stead. When they were on their mission, they could, within the guidelines, direct their own ministry. What a sense of importance they must have felt. Jesus trusted them with decision making and with the same kinds of tasks Jesus himself could do. To let the disciples control the process and independently make decisions did not encourage them to split from Jesus and go off on their own, but actually made them feel more loyal and more a part of the team.

Why? Because of the tremendous faith Jesus put in them. He needed them, and he let that be known through the very mission itself. People will much more readily follow a leader who lets them be involved and important, who respects their input and creativity. Leaders who hog the important tasks and recognition for themselves ultimately lose support.

The greatest compliment and respect you can pay to your followers is to depend on them.

14
HANDLING UNWANTED TASKS

"If any one forces you to go one mile, go with him two miles."

Matt. 5:41

This verse follows in the context of Jesus' discourse on loving your enemies and returning evil with good (Chapter 24 in this book). It's a curious verse for modern readers, but his audience would have understood him perfectly.

Jesus was not referring to kidnapping or hostage situations, as we in the twentieth century might assume. He is not recommending that hostages identify with the aggressor, as Patty Hearst appeared to do when she "joined" the Symbionese Liberation Army. His intent was really very different.

Palestine was under Roman domination in Jesus' day. The Roman army had numerous outposts in Palestine, which had to be continually supplied with provisions and matériel. Likewise, there was quite an efficient postal system operating, so mail had to be transported. Therefore, it was not uncommon, when the military was moving mail or supplies, to impress civilian travelers whom they spied along the way into service to help carry the load to its destination. Then the civilians were released. It didn't matter to the army if the civilians were inconvenienced or taken far out of their way. It was being temporarily impressed into service to which Jesus was most likely referring in Matthew 5:41.

What Jesus is really saying to today's workers is "If you are forced to carry out an unwanted assignment, do more than you are asked to do. Do it with excellent quality, diligence, and with a cheerful attitude, even if it takes you out of your way."

When you're forced by your boss or by the needs of the situation to carry out an unwanted assignment and you can't delegate it out, what are your options? You can

- grumble
- resist actively, refuse, and take the consequences
- beg off or procrastinate
- do it cheerfully

When push comes to shove, only the last option makes sense, unless, of course, the task would compromise your honor, values, or ethics. Then you should consider standing your ground and risk taking the ax with honor as opposed to knuckling under, dishonoring yourself, and feeling small and guilty later.

Assuming that the task in question will not compromise your values, it pays to tackle it with gusto. Why?

- *For your own sake.* A positive attitude makes it go faster, with less stress. Ever notice how tedious a task becomes when you make up your mind that you hate it? Mentally you wear out faster, physically you become more tense and fatigued. Your stress level rises. Is an unwanted task worth the personal strain?

  Besides, when you view a task negatively, your creativity shuts down and you become inefficient. This is especially true when anger sets in. You don't keep your mind on your task at that point. You're too busy feeling bad and thinking, "Poor me," or how to get even.

When you accept the task as an opportunity, however, it may open the door to broadening your skills or may even help you grow as a person. You can be more creative, as opportunity-thinking encourages you to consider new options.

- *For your followers' sake.* Remember how Tom Sawyer got Huckleberry Finn to whitewash the fence? You can effectively motivate others only when your personal energy is committed to the task. If you want the task out of the way quickly and easily, approach it cheerfully and encourage your followers to do their part the same way. A grumpy leader begets grumpy followers and destroys morale.
- *For your reputation's sake.* Jesus elsewhere makes the point that there is no honor or glory in giving to your friends, for even sinners do that. But to give to your enemies takes a special kind of person. The same is true here. Anyone can pitch in and accomplish a task he or she loves. But it takes a person of real quality to pursue with total commitment a task that one hates. By giving your all to an obnoxious task, you demonstrate your loyalty to the organization, you encourage the praise and trust of your supervisors, and you show your steadfastness and dependability to your followers. They all will come to have greater faith in you, which can open new networking and promotion possibilities. When faced with an unwanted-but-unavoidable assignment, never ignore the possible political and symbolic benefits that may accrue.

The moral of the story: "Go the extra mile."

15
CAPITALIZE ON TRADITION

Then Jesus came from Galilee to the Jordan to John, to be baptized by him. John would have prevented him, saying, "I need to be baptized by you, and do you come to me?" But Jesus answered him, "Let it be so now; for thus it is fitting for us to fulfill all righteousness." Then he consented.

Matt. 3:13–15

(*Parallel texts:* Mark 1:9–11; Luke 3:21, 22)

A new character emerges on the scene—John the Baptist. He was an ascetic, wandering preacher who lived in the desert, eating locusts and wild honey. Tradition holds that he was the son of Elizabeth, Jesus' mother's cousin. John preached a radical message of repentance and called his listeners to be baptized as a sign of their death unto sin and rebirth into a holy way of living. John was viewed by the political powers as a rabble-rouser, and indeed was beheaded by King Herod because he criticized him.

John was not unique. There were numerous preachers throughout Palestine, and even some who claimed to be the Messiah (see the Afterword for more details on the background of the times). At this particular time, there was a nationwide resurgence of religious fervor. More and more people were fed up with political and economic conditions and thus were turning to God for deliverance. After all, God had led the Israelites out of slavery from Egypt, and then generations later, he delivered them from exile in Babylon. Now people prayed for deliverance from Rome. Palestine was in a period of spiritual reawakening. What a perfect setting for Jesus to begin his public ministry. The timing could not be better.

Jesus' baptism was the kickoff for his public ministry. He was thirty years old, and we can assume that Jesus had been preparing himself spiritually and emotionally for this calling.

Baptism was a sign of repentance. Jesus, as Son of God, had no need of baptism or repentance. Jesus recognized this. In the non-canonical Gospel according to the Hebrews, we read, "The mother of the Lord and his brothers said to him, 'John the Baptist baptizes for the forgiveness of sins; let us go and be baptized by him.' But he [Jesus] said to them, 'In what way have I sinned that I should go and be baptized by him? Unless, perhaps, what I have just said is a sin of ignorance.' "

If Jesus was indeed sinless, why should he submit to baptism?

First of all, there were spiritual reasons. Jesus' baptism was the annunciation of his ministry, and reading on in Matthew, Mark, and Luke, we discover that, upon Jesus' rising from the water, a voice from heaven said, "This is my beloved son, with whom I am well pleased." God was giving Jesus his stamp of approval.

But there were also important tactical reasons.

First of all, Jesus was identifying with the people to whom he would ultimately preach. He was also showing his approval of and identification with the movement back to God. He was showing them that he was one of the people, not a preacher standing aloof and apart. Jesus was proving that he was not above doing what he asked others to do.

Luke 3:23 indicates that Jesus was about thirty years old when he began his ministry. Little is known of his life prior to his baptism. His father was a carpenter, and Jesus was the eldest son. It is generally assumed that Jesus spent these years in the traditional manner of the Jewish males of his day. He studied in the synagogue with his family and neighbors, and probably in his early teens he learned the carpentry trade from his father, practicing it until the time he began his ministry.

Jesus came from the people and identified with them throughout his ministry. He had lived a tradesman's life, not a princely one. He could empathize with the common person—his or her pains, dreams, hopes, and desires. Through being baptized by John, he made that identification apparent.

Also, his baptism was a public ritual. Jesus was a participant, apparently along with many other people. John was evidently a very popular and reasonably famous preacher. The Gospel of Mark speaks of all the people of Judea and Jerusalem going out to him. We could guess that on the day Jesus chose to be baptized, John was preaching to quite a crowd. Thus Jesus was taking a public stand with the people in their quest for a holier life.

Perhaps many of those to whom Jesus later preached were there at the River Jordan that day. Perhaps they would remember that Jesus also was baptized. His listeners saw the fact of his baptism as a common link with themselves; Jesus was not some noninvolved preacher pontificating from on high.

Identifying with the people you lead is always a critical strategy. This does not mean, however, that every leader in order to be effective must rise from the ranks of his or her followers. Often in the corporate world this is not the case. Key management is often hired from outside.

The point is that if the leader identifies with the followers, the followers are more likely to identify with the leader. People may follow a leader with whom they don't identify, but usually their heart and soul are not in it. We generally go the extra mile only for a leader whom we perceive as one of us, who cares for and understands us.

Up until the late eighteenth century, high military rank was usually bought by a wealthy man or given to an aristocrat in return for service to the crown. Those officers made it quite clear that they were a cut above—*well* above—the common soldier. In fact, they would rarely speak to the soldiers. They passed orders down to lieutenants, who would then talk to sergeants, who in turn actually commanded the rank and file. This system worked only because the general populace was taught to honor the nobility, and because military discipline was brutally strict. A minor infringement could bring forty lashes or even death.

Today the power of rule by fiat has worn exceptionally thin. People expect that promotion should be based on merit, that people in powerful positions should have earned the right to be there. We are suspicious of those who have bought, or wangled themselves through political maneuvering into, a leadership role. Equity is the key today. People rankle under obedience to the boss's son, unless the son has worked his way up.

Down deep, the same feeling was true in Jesus' day. People outwardly respected their standoffish and superior-acting religious leaders, but inwardly, many were critical. They would obey because they were supposed to, not because they wanted to. Many times Jesus criticized the religious establishment for their hypocrisy. Increasingly the people would rebel openly.

Jesus knew the psychology of leadership. He knew that it was not enough to get people to obey, but that he needed to win them over. To follow him out of love, not fear. And he knew that the first step in acquiring their love and devotion was getting them to identify with him as one of their own kind.

It doesn't matter whether you rise from the ranks or are imported into your leadership position from outside. The basic principle is the same. Work to build a strong identification with your people. Then they will begin to respond in kind.

Jesus did this in at least two ways in the account of his baptism.

First, he participated in the ritual itself, along with everyone else. He went where the people were. How often do leaders remain aloof? You may rarely see managers even enter the employees' cafeteria, let alone eat there, and if they do, they will often do it in small groups so that they can sit together, not having to share table space with the workers.

Are there certain activities at your company that managers never frequent? Certain places in the building where management never goes?

Jesus is saying by his baptism, "Break down those barriers. Go among the people, participate in their traditions."

Why doesn't management associate with workers? Because of company policy, because of tradition, to maintain "respect"? How often have you been told that in order to retain respect, you should keep distance between yourself and your followers? After all, the theory goes, power increases with greater mystery. If they know you too well, your power is diminished. This is only partly true.

Let's cut through the bull! The real reason for nonparticipation is *fear*! Fear that you will be seen as different, or that you won't know how to relate to them, and that they will reject you.

Start to participate, use the traditions of your organization to get to know your people. Perhaps you will lose some of the mystery, but you will gain a greater power—loyalty through identification.

Participating in your followers' or employees' organizational traditions and rituals is particularly important if you came from outside the company. By so doing, you identify yourself not only with the people, but with their organization, its history, and, by implication, its future goals.

Rituals and traditions, no matter how mundane they may appear on the surface, hold significant symbolic value for the employee, as has been spelled out in other chapters. Employees themselves may complain about some of them, but they will often resist management's attempts to change them. By participating, then, you are agreeing with and giving tacit support to the people. This identification at the symbolic level makes the bond even stronger.

What traditions or "rituals" exist in your organization that you can use as a bridge to bond you with your followers?

Secondly, Jesus went among the crowd that day at his baptism, and he was among the crowd ever after. He kept himself involved, close to the people whom he preached to and served.

Today Jesus would advocate "management by walking around," as long as while you walked, you interacted with and got to know the workers. Companies in which you will find the president getting his hands dirty on the shop floor have high productivity, higher loyalty, and less waste and turnover. This isn't because top management is spying on the workers. Far from it. The attitude from the top in such companies is one of trust and mutual participation and true commitment to company goals.

More and more we see evidence in excellently managed companies of flattening the pyramid, of management recognizing that its role is to support and be the resource for the workers. We're finally beginning to catch on to what Jesus was saying and doing two thousand years ago.

No matter what the product is that you create, you're in the people business. This fact eludes many managers, but the true leader counts on it.

16
TIMING AND DRAMA FOR IMPACT

And when they drew near to Jerusalem and came to Beth-phage, to the Mount of Olives, then Jesus sent two disciples, saying to them, "Go into the village opposite you, and immediately you will find an ass tied, and a colt with her; untie them and bring them to me. If any one says anything to you, you shall say, 'The Lord has need of them,' and he will send them immediately." This took place to fulfil what was spoken by the prophet, saying,

"Tell the daughter of Zion,
Behold, your king is coming to you, humble, and mounted
on an ass, and on a colt, the foal of an ass."

The disciples went and did as Jesus had directed them; they brought the ass and the colt, and put their garments on them, and he sat thereon. Most of the crowd spread their garments on the road, and others cut branches from the trees and spread them on the road. And the crowds that went before him and that followed him shouted, "Hosanna to the Son of David! Blessed is he who comes in the name of the Lord! Hosanna in the highest!"

Matt. 21:1–9

(*Parallel texts:* Mark 11:1–10; Luke 19:28–38;
John 12:12–15)

Jesus' Palm Sunday ride into Jerusalem was his greatest public statement to this point in his ministry. He had been preparing for it for three years. On several prior occasions, Jesus announced to his disciples that he would be going up to Jerusalem, the capital city. Now was the time, and everything most assuredly had been prepared in advance, with nothing left to chance.

The entry into Jerusalem was a well-crafted, symbolic, and dramatic event, carefully calculated to create an emotional and spiritual impact. Jesus had performed countless miracles and preached innumerable sermons. But in the act of entering Jerusalem, he sealed his claim on his Messiahship in a way that every religious Jew would understand.

Let's restructure the events and explore the symbolism Jesus used.

Jesus knew well the messianic prophecies, and his entry into Jerusalem was a direct fulfillment of two of them (Isa. 62:11 and Zech. 9:9), which Matthew blended together in his description of this event. It was the purpose of Matthew's Gospel to demonstrate Jesus' Messiahship, so throughout his Gospel, Old Testament prophecies are quoted, which Jesus was shown to have fulfilled.

How many, and what kind of, animals did Jesus ride? Mark, Luke, and John all refer to a colt. Matthew speaks of an ass and a colt. Who's right? Most likely, Jesus rode a young donkey. Mark and Luke state that the animal was never before ridden. Why does Matthew mention two animals? Ancient Hebrew poetry did not rhyme. Rather, its beauty and form lay in repetition or the restatement of the original phrase in different words. The Psalms are replete with such restatement. For example, "Deliver me, O Lord, from evil men; preserve me from violent men who plan evil things in their heart, and stir up wars continually" (Ps. 140:1, 2), and "I cry with my voice to the Lord, with my voice I make supplication to the Lord. I pour out my complaint before him, I tell my trouble before him" (Ps. 142:1, 2). The repetition was often added for emphasis, to add importance to the original statement. This is what Zechariah did in his original prophetic statement, which Matthew quotes. Apparently so that there would be no confusion, Matthew stated the facts of Jesus' entry to *literally* fulfill the prophecy; hence he has Jesus commanding that two animals be brought. Zechariah, however, referred to only one animal, and just used the second line, "on a colt, the foal of an ass," for poetic emphasis.

Today the ass is a lowly beast of burden; in fact, we even use the word *ass* as a put-down. In Jesus' day, however, the ass was considered a noble animal, necessary for daily life and commerce. In ancient times when a king would ride into a city he conquered, he would ride a white stallion. But when he came to the city on a mission of peace, he would ride an ass. The Messiah, prophesied in Zechariah, will enter and rule in peace; God will smite Israel's oppressors.

This symbolism was not lost to the crowd. They waved palm branches and shouted, "Blessed is the *King* who comes in the name of the Lord" (Luke 19:38a). They also shouted, "Hosanna," which means "Save us now." Clearly the people saw Jesus as the Messiah, who, in their minds, would drive out the Romans and bring peace to Israel.

Jesus had carefully orchestrated the event. Undoubtedly Jesus' disciples went into the town of Bethany to obtain the colt. Jesus had supporters there, and the use of the colt was obviously prearranged by Jesus.

Jesus' ride from Bethany to Jerusalem caused quite a stir. His reputation had preceded him. Long before this moment, Jesus "asked his disciples 'Who do men say that I am?' And they answered, 'John the Baptist; but others say, Elijah, and others, that one of the old prophets has risen' " (Mark 8:27b; Luke 9:19). Therefore we can imagine that the crowd of followers, curiosity seekers, and the hopeful oppressed grew and grew every mile of the way. Certainly people ran ahead announcing that Jesus was approaching. The crowd could have been in a frenzy, wild with expectation. Here was the Messiah, riding right into the seat of power. By the time Jesus reached Jerusalem, the crowds were waiting for him. His entry into the city was probably met with tumultuous excitement.

Jesus' timing was also carefully planned. He came to Jerusalem to celebrate the Passover, one of Judaism's highest and longest holy festivals. Passover celebrated the Israelites' redemption, their rescue from slavery in Egypt. What a perfect time, many of the spectators must have thought, for the Messiah to "take" Jerusalem and save Israel from the oppression of Rome.

His timing had more than symbolic impact, however. Judaism had many adherents and converts across the known world. At major celebrations such as Passover and Yom Kippur, Jerusalem's population swelled with thousands of pilgrims from all over Judea and throughout the Middle East who came to worship and celebrate at Solomon's Temple. If Jesus had wanted to launch a natural PR campaign through word of mouth, and get his message spread as far as possible, what better place and time could he have chosen? Everyone wants to be the first to share hot news. They just can't wait to tell their friends. Can you imagine these pilgrims and travelers telling all their friends when they returned home that they had seen, or perhaps even talked to or were touched by, the Messiah?

Jesus had built event upon event, symbol upon symbol, to drive home his claim to Messiahship. He carefully calculated and organized his activities during Holy Week, of which his entry in Jerusalem was the first. He timed his entry to have the greatest possible symbolic and reputation impact. His riding the donkey into Jerusalem was nothing short of a highly dramatic statement calculated to communicate a specific message.

What can you do to hammer home your point? Obviously, creating a parade as Jesus did is rarely appropriate for anyone except a political candidate. But you can do much to solidify your leadership and "market" your ideas by taking advantage of timing, drama, and local events.

Of course, you first need to determine your objective. What

do you wish to accomplish? What is the end result of your efforts that you wish to achieve? Now ask yourself these two questions from a different perspective: What do you want your followers or outside audience to *have in their minds*, and to *think and feel*, about you and your message?

Impact is not measured by what *you do*, but rather by what *they think and feel*. Creating impact, then, is the task of getting something new into the minds of others, or shifting what is already in their heads. People act in terms of how *they* think and feel, how *they interpret* what they see happening.

Therefore, when you design an activity for impact, your main consideration is not how you present it, but how they will receive it. When you create your impact strategy, then, determine your intended audience's needs, thoughts, and feelings. What things have meaning to *them*? It is around these issues that you choose your symbols and your actions.

All of this is so basic, so commonsense, so often ignored. Have you ever sat through a meeting where the boss or the head of the organization tried to motivate you to commit to the organizational goals, and it fell flat, nothing happened? I'd bet that nothing happened because the boss was talking about ideas that meant something to *him or her*, but meant little to the rank and file. It happens all the time.

Instead, discover the issues and symbols that are important and meaningful to your audience, and use those.

To summarize this point: (1) determine what you want to have happen in the minds and hearts of your audience (i.e., your ultimate objective), and (2) determine the symbols, issues, and actions to which they most strongly relate. Having done that, you incorporate those symbols and issues into your action plan. In fact, you may choose to build your action plan around those symbols and issues, as Jesus did.

Jesus wanted to celebrate the Passover in Jerusalem. He could have slipped in unnoticed in the teeming crowd of pilgrims and just rented a dining room. No. He needed to fulfill God's plan and state his claim to Messiahship. He knew the prophecies that the people longed to see fulfilled, and he planned and carried out his actions accordingly. Had he gone about his entry into Jerusalem a different way, the impact would probably not have been as great, and his message may have been confused. There was little confusion among the Palm Sunday crowd as to who Jesus was, because he used the key symbols his audience would understand.

As I'm writing this, I'm looking out my window at a sign on my neighbor's yard. It states the name of a local politician and the phrase "Finally a choice." The politician is trying to unseat the local incumbent in the state legislature. Her issue is abortion. She is pro-choice. Being a woman, trying to unseat a long-term male officeholder who came out vehemently as anti-abortion, she was not only hoping for the women's vote because she is female, but she was capitalizing on this hot national issue of abortion to give her the extra edge and develop a more passionate support. She won by a landslide.

Politicians use this tactic all the time. Why? Because it works.

If you have a message that you need to get across, why just say it? Why just say it over and over? Ask yourself how you can use timing and drama to give you the impact you need. This is the next step.

Once you've determined your ultimate objective and the symbols, issues, and actions to which your audience most strongly relates, you're ready to strategize your overall action plan. Here are the steps you may wish to use:

- Develop a time line. If there are specific steps you want to take, when must they all be completed? That's the end of your line. Then plot the intermediate activities that must occur in the proper order on the line, pegging down the dates upon which they must take place.
- Determine what the component activities will be. Must they coordinate with particular national, regional, or local events? If so, that will determine your timing. Tie into these wherever and whenever possible. If what you wish to do is indepen-

dent of external events, you are freer to create your own timing. In that case, you need to feel the pulse of your audience,
and build activity upon activity at the right pace for them to
accept and assimilate what you're doing. People outside your
organization often can advise you on *what to do*, but rarely
can they tell you *when*. You must develop your own sense of
timing by listening and networking with members of your
audience. This is especially true when you make organizational changes. Too rapid change confuses, hurts, and alien-
ates people. So do changes that are sprung on people or
changes for which the audience is inadequately prepared
even if appropriate notice is given.

• Develop dramatic ways to express your message. Don't rely
on words only. What *actions* can you do to get your point
across? Do you need to stage a rally? create a video? develop
and carry out a special ceremony?

Organizational consultant Terry Deal advocates the cre-
ation of a funeral ceremony for the old when major change is
incorporated into an organization. This helps people to let go,
to put the old system or organization to rest. It allows for the
mourning that so often needs to take place. Even if people are
gung-ho for the new, they still must work through their at-
tachment for the old, with its symbolic meanings. Terry Deal
has often found that if those old attachments are not recognized or addressed at a symbolic level, people are not as
ready to embrace the new, and the change is fraught with
much more difficulty.

At the divestiture of AT&T, Deal helped one AT&T division
to cope by creating a funeral for "Ma Bell." He helped the
employees to produce a video eulogizing "her." The employees themselves wrote the lyrics, created the poetry, wrote the
music, and staged and produced the whole project, and
starred in the resultant tape. The end result was a "funeral
service," at which the tape was played. That activity had
many component parts and involved numerous people. But
as they were creating the production, they were free to ex-

press their feelings for the old company and get them out, get past them. The overall transition was much easier for this unit because of this profound, symbolic production.

Naturally not all activities need to be so elaborate, but this is an example of what's possible. Brainstorm, ask friends or colleagues for ideas, especially friends in marketing, advertising, or public relations. Look for as many creative possibilities as you can. Be careful not to dismiss seemingly foolish or "impossible" ideas too quickly, for some of these may hold the key to your greatest impact potential.

• When the basic activities are chosen, hopefully with input from your followers and representatives of the intended audience, enlist their aid in carrying those activities out. Jesus let audience fervor help him spread his message. They became his ambassadors as they praised him and announced his coming. The audience wasn't passive; they became actively involved through their cheering. Your impact will be greater to the degree to which you can get your intended audience to actively participate. This hooks them emotionally, or better yet, they hook themselves at an emotional level with the message to the degree that they get involved.

What are you really doing? You're cementing your message firmly in the minds of your audience. They will never be able to relate to you and your message in the old ways again. That's the power of properly executed timing and drama. It may take careful planning and orchestration to accomplish, but the results will be worth it. And never forget that when we create a dramatic impact on others, we ourselves are more empowered as well!

17
REFRAME THE SYMBOLS

And he took bread, and when he had given thanks, he broke it and gave it to them, saying, "This is my body which is given for you. Do this in remembrance of me."

And likewise the cup after supper, saying, "This cup which is poured out for you is the new covenant in my blood . . .which is poured out for many for the forgiveness of sins."

> Luke 22:19,20; Matt. 26:28b
> (*Parallel texts:* Matt. 26:26–28; Mark 14:22–24;
> Luke 22:17–20; 1 Cor. 11:23–25)

Jesus was celebrating the first night of Passover with his disciples in Jerusalem on the eve of his execution. In two sentences, he completely redirected the meaning of Passover, redefining the context in terms of himself and his crucifixion. In so doing, he instituted the Sacrament of Holy Communion, the oldest and most universal of all rituals of Christendom.

Jesus' move was subtle, elegant, and sublime. Furthermore, it was extremely powerful in symbolizing Jesus' mission. In order to understand the power of Jesus' action, we need to take a brief look at God's Passover covenant with Israel.

The Book of Exodus describes how the Hebrews had become captives in Egypt. The time had come for God to deliver them, and bring them to the land He had promised to them. God called Moses and Aaron to lead the Hebrews out of Egypt, and sent them to Pharaoh to demand the Hebrews' release. God sent a series of plagues to Egypt to force Pharaoh's hand, the last of which was the killing of the firstborn of every family in Egypt.

God commanded that each Hebrew family kill a lamb and paint the blood on the doorposts and lintel. God would spare every family whose house was thus marked. On that night, the Hebrews were to eat that lamb and unleavened bread in preparation for their exodus the next day.

In God's plan, this sacrificial lamb became the substitute for the firstborn of Israel. Every family who sacrificed the lamb and displayed the blood on its door was saved. God also commanded that the Passover be celebrated forever to commemorate God's fulfilling of His covenant to lead His people out of bondage and into the Promised Land.

Jesus understood that his mission was to become the sacrifice, through his death, to free mankind from the bondage to sin. He was already aware that he would be betrayed that night and then crucified. In these two sentences, then, he defined himself as the lamb of a new parallel covenant, through whom God would forgive the sins of humanity. Jesus also commanded that his followers celebrate this Last Supper as a remembrance of Jesus' sacrificial act, and as a way of experiencing his presence after he was gone.

In strictly secular, tactical terms, what did Jesus do? He used one of the most holy and revered rituals of Judaism and redefined its meaning by symbolizing himself as the Paschal Lamb. He created a whole new interpretation with his sacrificial act as the center of the ceremony. This was a cognitive and emotional shift. To Jesus' immediate followers, who were Jewish, Passover could never be the same again. He used the Passover ceremony to drive home his mission in the minds and hearts of his adherents, and by using a powerful symbol, he gave his followers a means of remembering and commemorating his act down through the ages.

Futhermore, by selecting Passover as the original symbol, Jesus tied his mission and death directly to God, tradition, and history as the continuation and fulfillment of God's messianic covenant with Israel. The suffering and death of the Messiah had been prophesied in several places in the Old Testament. Thus the parallel with the original Passover in Egypt was just the symbolic tip of the iceberg, and his disciples would have well understood the much fuller, broader symbolic impact of the Last Supper, even though at that moment they could not fathom that Jesus was to be crucified. Had Jesus created an entirely new symbol rather than using Passover, the historic/theological link would have been lost.

Humanity thrives on its symbols. In fact, we couldn't survive as an advanced society without them. Stop and think about the myriad symbols to which we relate every day: the golden arches, the red circle and bar, which means "no," the handicapped parking sign, the flag, the national anthem, the cross. Symbols provide more than a verbal shorthand. Many are designed to evoke an emotional response, a tie to history, pride in our collective past and present. Symbols not only signify, they *unify*. Once such a symbol becomes ingrained in us emotionally, it becomes a very serious matter to change or tamper with it. Consider the recent furor over the issue of burning the American flag in protest. Also, at a recent convention a gentleman wore an American flag as a cape. and an audience of over twelve hundred loudly gasped in horror. We are intently loyal to our most cherished symbols; we rally around them, and we will fight, and even die, to preserve them.

For our purposes, we can identify two types of symbols. *Tangible* ones, which we can see, hear and touch, and *situational* ones, such as rituals, which we experience periodically. Often these intermingle. For example, a big banner with the company logo will be displayed at the annual awards ceremony. Symbols also have two forms of origin. They are either *created* specifically for their symbolic value, or they *evolve* into symbolic status over time.

Evolved symbols are the trickiest to define and manage. Whereas created symbols may have meaning throughout the whole organization, and are usually positive in nature, evolved symbols may be much more private, perhaps carrying meaning only for a small interest group. What's more, evolved symbols can be negative as well as positive. Negative ones rally certain folks *against* organizational objectives.

I was once called in to assist a major hospital to get one of its units to function cooperatively. There was tremendous dissension between the nursing staff and the unit director, an M.D., and he was totally baffled. When I interviewed a group of the nurses, one loudly blurted out, "They don't care about us." The rest chimed in, agreeing. When I asked how they came to this conclusion, which I knew to be false, the nurse said, "The monitors. They're always broken. We complain, but no one fixes them." In fact, the hospital had gone to great lengths to fix the monitors, but they still broke down. If the nurses were aware of the hospital's attempts, they chose to ignore them. The monitors had become a symbol to the nurses that they were undervalued. They had to use these monitors several times every day. Can you imagine what it must have felt like to see the monitor as a constant reminder of being taken for granted?

The unit director had no idea that the monitors were such a symbolic problem. He was advised to use the Jesus tactic. Once he recognized the symbolic value of the monitors as a negative symbol of his indifference to his nurses (which, to the nurses, symbolically placed him on the administration's side), he took on the monitor problem as his personal crusade. At the staff meetings he kept the nurses continually informed of his progress. The nurses began to make the cognitive/emotional shift. They began to feel grateful for his efforts. Finally, when the new monitors were installed, the unit director had red bows attached to each one! The symbol? "My gift to you. I care." Now whenever the nurses see and use those monitors, they remember how the director fought for their cause. The bows were an extremely powerful and vital symbolic addition. They marked victory, and a clear transition from old to new. The bows are now gone, but none of the nurses can ever forget them. While this did not solve all his problems with the nurses, the unit director gained great respect from the nursing staff over this issue, and made ultimate unit teamwork much easier to attain.

Evolved symbols can be very difficult to spot and can be actually very minor things. After the annual awards banquet of a large company, an employee went up to the president, pointed his finger at him, and growled, "You SOB." The president was astonished. The employee then said, "You served pie à la mode for dessert tonight. At these affairs we always had chocolate mousse!" Often it is the tiny, mundane changes that can affect people the most.

To use symbols to our advantage, we need to recognize them. While it's somewhat artificial, using the matrix below can help you identify the symbols operating in your organization.

	TANGIBLE	SITUATIONAL
CREATED	Logo, slogan Mission statement Office—locations within buildings Portraits, artwork Furnishings Other	Awards banquet Company picnic Staff meetings Other
EVOLVED	Watercooler Certain furnishings Certain apparatus Union contracts Other	An unresolved issue Certain procedures Traditional activities Certain meetings Other

Are there any symbols that you've identified that you could reframe or redefine to help you solidify your leadership position? Some symbols may be easier to redefine than others. Generally, created tangible symbols will be the hardest to alter, but if you become intimately identified with one or more of these, it can strongly enhance your position. For example, can you use your organization's slogan as a rallying point for a particular plan of action you wish to undertake? Can you redefine the meaning of the company logo to support your desired goals?

Let's pretend you work for a fictional company, Tigris Enterprises, whose logo is a capital T above a river, within a circle:

Suppose you wanted to kick off a new cooperative program there. You could tell the employees, "Whenever you see our giant T, think 'Together,' and the circle signifies our unity. Together, hand in hand, shoulder to shoulder, we will successfully navigate the river of success!" The more you yourself hammer home the symbolic redefinition, the more the followers will identify you with the new emphasis. On every follow-up memo you could write "T = together" or some other reminder. Symbols come to have meaning on their own. If you redefine them, you need to constantly reinforce that new meaning through repetition. Jesus knew this. That's why he said, "This cup is the new covenant in my blood. Do this, *as often as you drink it*, in remembrance of me" (1 Cor. 11:25b).

Perhaps easier to directly modify are the evolved situational symbols, as accomplished by the hospital unit director. Here the major detective work is in discovering what these symbols

actually are and how they are viewed by your potential followers. Don't forget that, if you tackle an unresolved issue, there
may be strong political factors involved, and there may even be
secret opponents who will block such an issue's resolution. If
you tackle such an issue, you face Charlie Brown's perpetual
dilemma—you could wind up the hero or the goat. Greater
glory often carries greater risk. Beware. Examine the ramifications before going out on a limb.

Symbols are powerful. Use them strategically.

- First determine your ultimate objective.
- Determine if a symbolic identification will further your cause.
- If so, which symbol(s) should you use? While picking the
  right one can enhance your position, in some cases picking
  the wrong one can do you in.
- How could the symbol be best used or redefined? This is a
  critical question and should not be answered in haste. Think
  it all through, plan it out, and even check it out with a mentor,
  career coach, or some other knowledgeable, neutral person.
- Carefully plan the timing and manner of your introduction of
  the redefined symbol to your followers, especially if you are
  going to make a formal presentation. Jesus used his *last* Passover to institute Holy Communion. The timing was tied to his
  betrayal and crucifixion. This ceremonial act, if done at a
  Passover three years earlier, would have had little impact.
- Get all supporting materials and people lined up beforehand.

In short, if you want to win, you have to *prepare* to win. Also,
an ounce of prevention is worth a pound of cure. Never under-
estimate the power of symbols to aid your cause. That's why
they must be handled carefully, with savvy.

Many managers take on leadership positions and never think
about the symbols at their disposal, nor the symbolic impact of
their own leadership position, for that matter. Yet an understanding of the symbolic aspects of organizations is essential,
because most interpersonal difficulties that managers don't

know how to solve have their causes in the symbolic or political spheres. By actively understanding and using the symbols with which your followers already identify, you open a whole new dimension and power to your leadership capability and style.

18
REDEFINE THE LAW

"You have heard that it was said to the men of old, 'You shall not kill; and whoever kills shall be liable to judgment.' But I say to you that every one who is angry with his brother shall be liable to judgment."

Matt. 5:21, 22a

"You have heard that it was said, 'An eye for an eye and a tooth for a tooth.' But I say to you, do not resist one who is evil."

Matt. 5:38, 39a

"Again you have heard that it was said to the men of old, 'You shall not swear falsely, but shall perform to the Lord what you have sworn.' But I say to you, do not swear at all. "

Matt. 5:33, 34a

What is Jesus doing? In these passages and others from his Sermon on the Mount, Jesus is giving a discourse on appropri-

---

ate moral living. He is reaffirming the commandments and Levitical principles. In the wilderness, Moses gave the Israelites the Ten Commandments and numerous other laws for conduct and worship, which the priests and Levites had been interpreting and teaching to the people ever since. Is Jesus just doing the same thing?

Read these passages carefully. Jesus is really doing something much more powerful than just giving a moral discourse. He is actually redefining the law. Notice his technique. He does this numerous times in quick succession, at the beginning and throughout the early part of his Sermon on the Mount: "You have heard it said . . . But I say to you . . ." Jesus states the basic principle, and then reinterprets it in a more broad, all-inclusive, or stringent way. He redefines the law in such a way that he is setting himself up as the authority, a greater authority than the priests and scribes who preceded him. Jesus' use of the phrase "But I say to you" implies an opposition to what has been said in his preceding sentence, as if the original principle that he was discussing is insufficient, or in some cases, downright wrong.

This was a powerful move. In Jesus' day, to the religious Jew, the law was sacred. The rabbis had a saying, "Nothing is good but the Law." You could discuss the fine points of the law, but you were not free to change it. The Pharisees prided themselves on obeying the law to the letter. This was, after all, the divine law, given by God to Moses, the Israelites' greatest prophet. Now here comes Jesus, stating that the prior interpretations of the law were inadequate. Can you imagine the ire of some of his listeners? Some may have said to each other, "He sets himself up as greater than Moses!" Most of his listeners were captivated by his message and impressed with the authority with which he spoke: "And when Jesus finished these sayings the crowds were astonished at his teaching, for he taught them as one who had authority, and not as their scribes" (Matt. 7:28, 29).

His listeners were amazed, not only at what he said but also at how he said it. He commanded their attention and respect through his "presence," and also through technique.

It was no accident that he used the formula "You have heard it said . . . But I say to you . . ." near the opening of the sermon. Likewise, it is not by chance that he happened to repeat that formula several times over during the early part of his sermon. He was stating his authority in this manner right from the beginning and hammered it home again and again.

The technique is simple to use but awesome in its power, when used with a potent message delivered in courageous style. You can use it to your advantage, too. When you want to make a powerful point, state it as an extension or broadened application of something your followers already believe in and respect. Perhaps that something is a basic principle from the Bible, the Constitution, or your corporate mission statement. Turn it around in a way that is consistent with the original meaning (or, if you're particularly daring, opposed to the original meaning), using it as the basis and also the context for your point.

Here are a couple of sample speech openers:

> Abraham Lincoln, in his famous Gettysburg Address, stated that "government of the people, by the people, and for the people, shall not perish from the earth." But I say to you that this powerful nation *will* perish unless our people begin to take on the responsibility for their own destiny.

> The Statue of Liberty has emblazoned on its base the founding principle of this nation: "Give me your tired, your poor, your huddled masses yearning to breathe free." Today, I'm telling you, those huddled masses need more. They need opportunity—to build, to create, to take their part in making this nation great.

The implication in the above examples is that the speaker is equal to or even more correct than Abraham Lincoln, the Statue of Liberty, or the Founding Fathers. This puts the speaker in a powerful position indeed.

There is one caveat, however. If you use this technique in a public address or even in informal conversation, its power gives you a high profile. You've come out and taken a stand on an important issue or principle. Therefore, you have to be consistent and back it up with your actions, lest you be seen as a hypocrite and destroy your credibility. This is not a technique for the cautious, but when you really have something to say, this method will deliver it with impact.

Likewise, this is not a technique for the egocentric. If too much emphasis is put on the "I" in the formula, you might appear pompous. Be careful not to overemphasize the "I," and let the technique itself carry the authority. It will, if the passion and vocal energy are there.

Of course, it is not necessary to use Jesus' formula in order to redefine the law. Nor is this technique limited only to the spoken word. It works well in writing also. The example in the last chapter of creating a new interpretation to the Tigris Enterprises logo falls into this category. You could do the same with personnel policy, corporate slogans, symbols, or logos—anything in your organization with which your followers would be familiar and for which they have respect.

Of course, it goes without saying that you shouldn't go around looking for something to redefine just to assert power or authority. The technique, when used, should be an integral part of a point you are trying to drive home.

Jesus used the technique in the context of preaching the message that a strictly literal, outward adherence to the law was insufficient. One also had to follow the law in one's heart. Jesus was pressing for a moral, attitudinal change, with a call for improved behavior. The technique works especially well when this kind of change is called for, when you want people to stop taking familiar principles for granted. It works when you want to breathe new life into a familiar tradition or idea. It's powerful when you want to add a new twist to a cherished concept.

The technique is not only powerful in asserting authority. It is a simple but potent learning device. People learn by association. In Psychology 101, you learned how Pavlov taught his dogs to salivate to the sound of a bell by ringing the bell when he presented them with meat. This is direct-association learning. You do the same when you link your new interpretation to an idea, symbol, phrase, or statement with which your listeners are already familiar. Whenever they think of the original symbol, your new interpretation will come to their minds. Do your job well, and they will never be able to think about the original symbol or idea in the same way again.

Power is the ability to influence. Influence is causing change in the way people think. Proper and positive use of Jesus' method will do it.

19
THE POWER OF REVERSE PSYCHOLOGY

And there came a man named Jairus, who was a ruler of the synagogue; and falling at Jesus' feet he besought him to come to his house, for he had an only daughter, about twelve years of age, and she was dying. As he went, the people pressed round him. . . .While [Jesus] was still speaking, a man from the ruler's house came and said, "Your daughter is dead; do not trouble the Teacher any more." But Jesus on hearing this answered him, "Do not fear; only believe, and she shall be well." And when he came to the house, he permitted no one to enter with him, except Peter and John and James, and the father and mother of the child. And all were weeping and bewailing her; but he said, "Do not weep; for she is not dead but sleeping." And they laughed at him, knowing that she was dead. But taking her by the hand he called, saying, "Child, arise." And her spirit returned, and she got up at once; and he directed that something should be given her to eat. And her parents were amazed; but he charged them to tell no one what had happened.

Luke 8:41, 42, 49–56

(*Parallel texts:* Matt. 9:18, 19, 23, 26; Mark 5:22–24, 35–43)

Was Jesus crazy? Jairus was a ruler of the synagogue. If he wasn't wealthy, he certainly was one of the most well-known and influential men in town. By the time Jesus and his disciples arrived at Jairus's house, the child had died and the professional mourners and family had been summoned. Jesus had to wend his way through a small crowd. Privately, in front of only a few chosen disciples and the girl's parents (Mark 5:40), Jesus raised her from the dead. The crowd of mourners and the rest of the family were just on the other side of the door. And Jesus tells the parents to tell no one of this? How could such a secret be kept?

Jesus frequently performed miracles, and then told the people to tell no one. What's going on? If the lame start walking, the blind suddenly see, a girl who the whole town knew was dead is now outside playing in her yard, the events speak for themselves. With Jesus' superb understanding of human behavior, why would he be so foolish as to expect that people could keep such a powerful secret?

Jesus *didn't* expect them to keep quiet. In fact, he *counted* on the fact that no sooner would he turn his back than his miraculous "secret" would be spread all over town.

Now, elsewhere in the Gospels, it is rationalized that people were to keep his healings and other miracles secret because his time had not yet come. In other words, he was not ready yet for his identity as the Messiah to be made known. That information, if told to the recipient of the miracle, would make the secret even sweeter to tell.

Everyone loves to tell a secret, for a couple of reasons. First, there is a certain excitement in telling something that has been forbidden to be told. Generally, something that is naughty is seen as being more fun than something that is not. The fact that Jesus had forbidden them to spread the news actually added impetus to their natural desire to tell others what had happened. There's no fun in spreading common knowledge.

Secondly, knowledge provides power and status. If I tell you a secret, then you are "in the know." You're special, and to that degree, you are one up on those who are not let in on the information. Now compound those feelings with the heightened status you would have if a famous or important person were to confide in you with secret information. The very fact that the information is a secret boosts your importance and your specialness. If the "secret" were not private at all, but common knowledge, the special status would be lost.

Have you ever told a friend a secret, only to find out that the friend already knew? You couldn't wait to tell, and when your friend said, "Oh, I heard *that* a week ago!" remember how crestfallen you felt? See what I mean about status?

Now, here's the rub. A secret is of no value if you keep it! If you keep your mouth shut, no one else knows that you have the intimate knowledge. There is no status payoff for you until you break your silence. Only then may you have your moment of glory. When you tell your secret, you pass on the opportunity to your friend, and now he or she gets a chance for the same status in telling the next person. We love to hear secrets, not just to find out private scuttlebutt but so that we can have the thrill of gossiping and passing it on.

But there is another reason why secrets are important. They make us feel *included*. They can bond us together through the shared possession of private knowledge. The Masons and other secret societies throughout history have used secret initiations, rites, rituals, and information to draw people together, to set "us" apart from "them." Having this knowledge, we as the in-group feel special. Having secret information, and therefore the responsibility for keeping it secret, is a very powerful motivator and ego enhancer indeed.

So by telling the common folk who received or witnessed his miracles to keep secret what happened, Jesus accomplished two very important things. First, it bonded them with himself. It elevated them and made them feel important. How special they must be if the Messiah told them, "Don't tell anyone. This is just between us." Secondly, it *guaranteed* that his reputation would spread like wildfire.

At a deeper level, telling secrets reflects an oppositional, rebellious attitude. People who tell secrets are actually betraying the person who exhorted them to keep quiet. They are using the private knowledge, and therefore the person who told them the secret or the persons whom the secret is about, for their own emotional gain. Of course, at some level that oppositional attitude is possessed by us all. We are all guilty of breaching minor confidences. However, the chronic gossip, who "just can't keep a secret," actually has a lust for status and power. He or she must be the center of attention and also one up, and spills secret knowledge to get there. Such a person is really a user and soon convinces people that he or she can't be trusted.

Psychotherapists are quite aware of this basic oppositional tendency. There is a psychotherapeutic technique called "prescribing the symptom," in which the patient is told to actively engage in, or even exaggerate, the very behavior he or she is trying to eliminate. Handled deftly by the therapist, this technique reduces the problem behavior. Why? First of all, the problem behavior itself reflects the patient's subconscious oppositional attitude toward others. When the therapist tells the patient to go ahead, do the problem behavior, such as getting more anxious or depressed, the patient is placed in a double bind. If he obeys, then he ceases to rebel. If he disobeys the therapist, then his symptoms improve.

Secondly, when the symptom is prescribed, the patient is faced with the fact that his problem behaviors are directly under his own control. This is the very fact that, by creating "symptoms," he has been subconsciously trying to deny. If he in any way alters his symptomatic behavior at the suggestion of the therapist, he can no longer deny his role as creator of the problem. Since that would be too uncomfortable for his ego to handle, he begins to improve.

Psychiatrist Alfred Adler once used a similar technique on an insomniac, which other psychotherapists have also used with success. A patient once complained that he couldn't sleep, whereupon Adler said, "Since you can't sleep, why waste your time worrying about your loss of sleep? Rather, lie awake in the bed and think of all the ways in which you can make other people happy." From then on, the patient slept like a log!

Reverse psychology, "paradoxical intention," prescribing the symptom: these are extremely potent techniques. To pull them off successfully, without their backfiring on you, takes a high level of sensitivity and savvy as to how people tick, and superb ability to evaluate the circumstances and internal motivations involved. Books have been written on this vast and diverse subject, so it's far beyond the scope of this small book to delve into the how-tos. If you feel that reverse psychology techniques would help you, then check with your local library for added information. But don't try these methods if you're not sure you have the people-knowledge and empathy to manage it.

Using reverse psychology is a high-risk gamble. Win, and you can win big; lose, and you lose it all—your credibility and your reputation. Nothing is worse for a leader than to be seen as a manipulator, to be caught "techniquing" people. Dishonesty is the worst blotch your reputation could suffer, and one from which you will not readily recover.

It goes without saying that when Jesus used these methods, he was completely honest and aboveboard. He wasn't manipulating people, but rather he was counting on human nature to work in a particular way. Also, while I have touched the idea of reverse psychology in general, Jesus' main use of it was in one primary area—the telling of secrets. This is one area that you may legitimately pursue with relatively little risk if it's appropriate to your situation.

First, ask yourself if possessing and dealing with private information is part of your group's normal function. For some groups in some settings, such as a personnel department or a research lab, private information is commonplace, and often must be kept confidential. This is not private information that is to be "used" in the sense of keeping a secret or bonding.

Rather, the secret information that concerns us is "hot news," "inside dope," or insights of yours that you would share with your followers. By releasing this information, you bring them even more into your inner circle and elevate them to a more psychologically equal status because they now know what you know.

You need to make a distinction between the information that you really need your followers to hold confidential and that which you really want leaked out. This means being careful to discern the nature of the information, but also how well you can trust your followers to keep a confidence. Generally, trustworthy followers will keep appropriate information quiet.

"Don't tell anyone, but . . ." is a good line to use when you really want information spread. "This isn't for public knowledge" or "The announcement hasn't been made yet, but . . ." are also effective ways to drop into the rumor mill positive information about your, or your group's, accomplishments.

Often, to solidify your position, the only thing worse than being talked about is not being talked about. By judiciously dropping "secrets" at appropriate times, you can guarantee that that illicit PR network, the "office grapevine," is yielding you a full harvest.

20
"JUDGE NOT"

"Judge not, that you be not judged. For with the judgment
you pronounce you will be judged, and the measure you
give will be the measure you get. Why do you see the speck
that is in your brother's eye, but do not notice the log that
is in your own eye? Or how can you say to your brother,
'Let me take the speck out of your eye' when there is the
log in your own eye? You hypocrite, first take the log out of
your own eye, and then you will see clearly to take the
speck out of your brother's eye."

Matt. 7:1–5

(*Parallel text:* Luke 6:37, 41, 42)

Early in the morning he came again to the temple; all the
people came to him, and he sat down and taught them. The
scribes and the Pharisees brought a woman who had been
caught in adultery, and placing her in the midst they said
to him, "Teacher, this woman has been caught in the act of
adultery. Now in the law Moses commanded us to stone
such. What do you say about her?" This they said to test

him, that they might have some charge to bring against him. Jesus bent down and wrote with his finger on the ground. And as they continued to ask him, he stood up and said to them, "Let him who is without sin among you be the first to throw a stone at her." And once more he bent down and wrote with his finger on the ground. But when they heard it, they went away, one by one, beginning with the eldest, and Jesus was left alone with the woman standing before him. Jesus looked up and said to her, "Woman, where are they? Has no one condemned you?" She said, "No one, Lord." And Jesus said, "Neither do I condemn you; go, and do not sin again."

John 8:2–11

How often have we quoted to someone else, "Judge not that you be not judged," using a judgmental tone?

Judging others is the easiest thing in the world to do. It boosts our egos, making us feel important when we can find fault in someone else. In that moment we delude ourselves into thinking that we are better than they are. Criticism, perfectionism, and faultfinding are a way of life for some people. Most of us are pretty good at it. Judging others may be the most pervasive and pernicious sin of all.

What are we doing when we judge others? First of all, we are setting ourselves up as the authority, as if *we*, or the standards *we* espouse, are the rule by which the world should run. Honestly now, isn't the practical definition of "perfect" actually "the way I would have done it"?

We do this to elevate ourselves in our own minds. Now, who of us need to elevate ourselves? Those with low self-esteem. Those who feel lousy about themselves are the ones who boost their own egos by finding greater fault in others. If they can't raise themselves, at least they can get ahead comparatively by putting others lower. Those with good self-esteem have little need to rise above others. They enjoy recognition, all right. But they feel good enough about themselves in their own right that they need not think competitively nor judge their worth relative to others. Such people do not need to take upon themselves a prerogative that rightfully belongs to God.

Secondly, we judge others to belittle them. In this case, the main motivation is to attack. It reflects our anger, our basic hostility. Anger, however, is a superficial emotion. There is always something else that lies behind it. Usually we don't feel angry unless we are feeling hurt or out of control. Then we use anger to get even or to shift the balance of power back into our favor by intimidating others. Either we or our egos can suffer the hurt. Either way, being judgmental is a passive-aggressive way of acting out in response.

Judging in anger is often a reflection of another, more insidious motive—jealousy. When we're jealous of someone, our ego can't rest till it knocks the person down to size. In truth, no one is comfortable too long with the idea that someone else is superior. We can accept someone else's occasional superior accomplishment, but should she win regularly, we often find ourselves harboring enmity about her in our hearts. We can accept a person's holding a superior post at work, such as manager or supervisor. But how quick we are to pounce on any little mistake he makes if we think his position has gone to his head.

We often justify our judgmentalism with "righteous indignation" or "constructive criticism." Sadly, however, there is rarely anything righteous in indignation, and very little that is constructive in criticism. Yet we whitewash our actions and feelings to the point that when we judge, we think that we are being holy, or worse yet, wholly helpful.

Where do we get this tendency to judge? It's all around us. Everyone's doing it. We cut our teeth on criticism from birth. Our parents and older siblings taught us the fine art of criticism through applying it to us, and society has reinforced it ever since.

We live in a mistake-oriented society. In our homes, schools, workplaces, on the playing field, even in our houses of worship, the mistakes we make often count much more than our accomplishments in determining how we are evaluated. In fact, a thousand successes often can't make up for one mistake. So conditioned are we to notice the wrong and overlook the right.

Our grades, our performance reviews, most of the ways by which we formally evaluate others, focus foremost on errors, even though we honestly may wish to help people overcome their difficulties. Is it any wonder then, that criticism—judgment—is often the first thing we do even when trying to help, counsel, guide, and assist others?

The end result of judging is discouragement. We are often discouraged ourselves—that's why so often we feel the need to judge others. And when we judge, we discourage those on the receiving end. People may accept being helped, but they never are comfortable with being judged. Yet we've lulled our minds into thinking that when we judge people, they will be so thrilled to receive that information that they will rush right out and correct the error of their ways! Wrong! They will feel put down, will harbor resentment, and look for ways to even the score.

Judging others is like demolishing a house of cards. You judge someone—you put her down. She tries to get even by knocking or hurting you. You and she act out your respective discouragement by judging others, who resent you both in return. Knock down one card and the whole house goes to smithereens.

For what? Is the supposed gain worth the pain? There is one common denominator to the vast majority of mental illness, emotional upset, poverty, crime, prejudice, sexual and racial harassment, and chronic dropouts and dissatisfaction of all kinds, along with drug, alcohol, food, and other substance abuse. In fact, these "problems" I've just listed are not the problems, but the *answers* people have chosen to cope with the real problem—discouragement. The discouraged person is out of touch: (1) with himself—self-esteem and feelings of personal worth are low, self-criticism is high; (2) with others—by not feeling worthwhile, he feels less than others, lonely and out of place, regardless of how affable and friendly he may appear on the surface; and (3) with God—he feels cut off from God's grace and has erected a self-imposed barrier to experiencing His love. And the chronic, lifelong receiving and giving of judgments is a key element in setting the downward spiral of discouragement in motion.

Jesus knew all about the effects of judgment. Routinely he pricked the ego balloons of hypocrisy. He recognized that to judge others is one of the most insidious, undermining things one human being could do to another, because it undercuts self-worth. Jesus knew that what goes around comes around; that if we want to escape being condemned ourselves, we had better not condemn others.

How did Jesus handle judgment? In the first passage quoted, Jesus puts the whole issue into perspective. For someone to judge anyone else on anything, Jesus says, is hypocrisy. Unless you're perfect, he's saying, you've got no business judging anybody else for any reason. If you judge your partner for a sin that you deem to be severe, who's to say that you haven't committed another sin even more grievous? Therefore, what gives you the right to judge? Judging is really God's prerogative; we have no business being in the judging business, or infringing upon God's territory. And how, or whether, God judges is up to Him.

In the second passage we see an example of ultimate compassion. Let's look at what was going on. By this time, the religious leaders were threatened by Jesus' reputation. They saw Jesus as their adversary, and so they were out to get him. While Jesus was teaching in their vicinity, they picked up a nameless woman who was caught in the act of adultery. Jewish law stated that the punishment for adulterous women was death by stoning. This woman's life was on the line, and here she was, a pawn in a showdown between Jesus and the religious leaders. It is clear that the scribes and Pharisees cared not one wit for this woman. She was an object to them, a tool for their own use. She did not exist as a person in any meaningful way for the religious leaders. They gave her neither pity nor consideration as a person. "After all," they probably reasoned, "she committed a crime and deserves to die. Who cares about compassion or circumstances? She broke the law."

Jesus saw through their ruse and turned the issue back on them in a unique way. His words were a mirror for their hearts and souls, and we can picture them, one by one, with head hung low, slipping silently and shamefully away.

Jesus' real compassion shows through in how he handled the woman. There was no question about her guilt. She was caught in the act. Jesus refused to condemn her; rather, he forgave her. He wasn't saying that it was okay to sin. Jesus wasn't taking the sin lightly, as some readers of John's text might believe. What he did do was to accept her worth as a person. He did not condemn nor reprove her. This would have been a marvelous opportunity for Jesus to deliver a private lecture on sexual morality, but he didn't. He forgave, showing his mercy.

But Jesus didn't let her off easily. He threw down a challenge: "Go and sin no more." She came within an inch of her life, and got a second chance. What was she going to do with it? Would she go back to her old ways, or would she, like many who have a close brush with death, turn over a new leaf? No one knows. What we do know is that, while Jesus forgave her, he still held her accountable. He wasn't saying, "So what?" to her adultery. Rather he commanded her not to do it again.

Jesus' command was actually a statement of encouragement. He would not have told her to sin no more if he didn't think she could do it. He didn't mean for her to be perfect. No human can achieve that. Rather, he told her to turn her life around, make wiser, more moral and holy choices, do that which is right and proper. Jesus' comment showed the woman that he had faith in her. Faith that she would make good use of her second chance.

What can you as a leader draw from these passages?

Judgment and empowerment are mutually exclusive. Judging undermines people's power. Clearly, judging your followers for their errors is inappropriate. If that's the case, how can we cope with mistakes that need correcting?

We all make mistakes; we all must be corrected at times. But that's not judging. Never confuse judgment with feedback. Judgment is a statement about the person; feedback is a statement about the behavior.

- Give feedback in nonjudgmental terms. Talk about the actions that caused the difficulty; never disparage the person. Be careful not to use pejorative terms, such as "stupid" or "foolish," even about the actions, as emotionally laden words will be received as an attack.

- Be firm but kind. Curb your anger. Put off dealing with the issue until you can do so in a calm manner. Let it be known that change must be made.

- Focus on strengths. Look at the resources that people have to improve. Emphasizing the positive not only helps people discover creative solutions, but also helps to encourage and soothe any hurt or loss of face they may have suffered.

- Hold them accountable for improved behavior. Forgiveness does not mean that people are let off the hook. Show them that you have faith in their ability to improve or rectify the situation.

- Provide assistance where necessary, either through direct or indirect help or by showing emotional support. Hang in there for them, and encourage them to come to you for help whenever needed, showing them that there is no shame in seeking appropriate assistance.

All of this shows that you *care*, and that is the most empowering, encouraging act of all.

For all of this to work, however, requires that you not only act nonjudgmentally, but that you develop a *nonjudgmental attitude*. Trust is a key issue. If you're judgmental, people won't trust you. They won't own up to their mistakes but will hide them. Remember that admitting a fault is just about the hardest thing for most of us to do, slightly harder than leaping across the Grand Canyon with a single bound! That's true even in an accepting environment, so consider how much harder it would be to face up to your errors in a setting in which you felt attacked.

A nonjudgmental attitude looks to forgive. It sees beyond the person to the circumstances, to the possibility of hidden contingencies and pressures on the person, of which you may never become aware. It promotes understanding, empowerment, and love as the basis of decision making. It is positive and encourages improved action and attitude on the part of those who err. It refuses to make excuses for misbehavior.

A judgmental attitude, on the other hand, seeks first to punish. The person gets lost in the act. Hostility and low self-esteem lie at its roots, so how can it ever help people grow? Indeed it stunts growth, and encourages distrust and hostility.

If none of this makes sense from an altruistic point of view, then consider letting go of judgment for purely self-protective reasons. What goes around comes around. If you judge others, setting yourself above them, rest assured they will even the score, looking to topple your pedestal. They will search diligently to discover all your teeny-weeny mistakes, and gleefully relish them when they find them. Others will develop a hostile and rebellious attitude toward you, and you will lose your credibility and power with your people. And like the Pharisees and scribes in this incident of old, you might, when confronted, be driven off the field, your head bowed in shame.

By abandoning judgment and its handmaiden, perfectionism, you actually enhance your power. People will be drawn to you because your attitude of acceptance is so rare and refreshing in their experience, and so empowering. You will earn their loyalty. And when the game is over, you can walk off the field with your head held high, your team solidly behind you.

21
MANAGING THE SUPERSTARS

And James and John, the sons of Zebedee, came forward to him, and said to him, "Teacher, we want you to do for us whatever we ask of you." And he said to them, "What do you want me to do for you?" And they said to him, "Grant us to sit, one at your right hand and one at your left, in your glory." But Jesus said to them, "You do not know what you are asking. Are you able to drink the cup that I drink, or to be baptized with the baptism with which I am baptized?" And they said to him, "We are able." And Jesus said to them, "The cup that I drink you will drink; and with the baptism with which I am baptized, you will be baptized; but to sit at my right hand or at my left is not mine to grant, but it is for those for whom it has been prepared." And when the ten heard it, they began to be indignant at James and John. And Jesus called them to him and said to them, "You know that those who are supposed to rule over the Gentiles lord it over them, and their great men exercise authority over them. But it shall not be so among you; but whoever would be great among you must be your servant, and whoever would be first among you must be slave of all. For the Son of man also came not to be served but to serve, and to give his life as a ransom for many."

Mark 10:35–45

(*Parallel texts*: Matt. 20:20–28; Luke 22:24–27. See also Luke 10:17–20)

Here again the issue comes up: what to do with the ego. It might be helpful to review Chapters 3 and 4 at this point. In this chapter, however, we take a different tack—how to handle the egocentric, especially one with a talent or other attribute to back it up.

Superstars are a real thorn in the side of any coach. What do you do with them, and depending on the circumstances, what could you do without them? Superstars are rarely team players. They may serve on the team, but will often purposefully outshine their teammates or perform in other ways at the team's expense so that they will get special recognition or reward. In short, they often will hog the glory that rightfully should have been shared.

Superstars often can put us into a bind. On the one hand they challenge our egos. If they perform in a consistently superior way, we may feel threatened. We may respond with animosity, especially if the superstar acts in a haughty manner. Often this animosity is a cover for our basic jealousy of these people and of what they are able to accomplish. When this happens, down deep we want to squash them, or see them get their comeuppance. Often we will want to challenge them in a clash of the titan egos.

On the other side of the coin, we may see the superstars as carrying the hopes of the team. When this is the case, we are apt to appreciate them too much. We may rely upon their efforts and skills at a disproportionately high level in comparison to the capabilities and talents of the rest of the team.

While we as leaders may appreciate the superstars, you can bet your bottom dollar that their teammates don't. Teammates can be legitimately pleased and impressed if one of their number distinguishes him- or herself in a particular way, but should this same person achieve this consistently, teammates' pride can turn to envy and even to hatred. Such was the case with Cain's feelings toward Abel, with Joseph's brothers' attitude toward Joseph, and it occurs all too frequently today. It gets chilly working constantly in someone else's shadow. We all want the warm glow of recognition to shine on our faces, and our sense of "fair play" suggests that, on a team, we all should have an equal shot at it.

Thus superstars can destroy teamwork—and tempt us sorely as leaders.

If we challenge them or spar with them in an ego clash, we end up creating a battlefront where the other, less-recognized teammates may side with us. But have we won anything? We might have won the battle, but we will surely lose the war, if for no other reason than that the teamwork we would need to accomplish our mission is ultimately destroyed. Look what happened when King Arthur waged war on Sir Lancelot. Arthur's dream of Camelot and the virtues of the Round Table were completely obliterated.

If we rely too heavily on our superstars' talents, teamwork is also destroyed for the reasons described above. Yet it's so tempting to use what these people have to offer. If we don't use them to full capacity, or try to hold them back, they will get disgruntled. And if we do use them fully, we court the envy of their teammates.

Clearly, superstars put us between a rock and a hard place. They must be managed. What can we do?

Jesus was faced with this issue more than once among his disciples. In the Mark account that opened this chapter, we see James and John saying in effect, "Please do us a favor. Let each of us have a special place in the kingdom." (In the Matthew parallel, which we referenced in Chapter 4, it was James and John's mother who made this request for her sons.)

James and John probably had a special relationship with Jesus. John referred to himself in his Gospel as "the disciple whom Jesus loved." It is also quite possible that James and John were actually Jesus' cousins. It might have been very tempting for Jesus to grant their request, but he handled the situation very adroitly.

We don't know how Jesus felt in this situation. The Gospel accounts are silent about that. We do know, however, that whatever his instant reaction, he did not yield to the temptation of the moment.

He could have given James and John a real verbal dressing down, lambasting them for their impudence and misplaced ambition, and not being good team players. He could have criticized them for trying to capitalize on their family connection with Jesus. He could have made an example of them. That certainly would have satisfied the remaining ten indignant disciples. But Jesus didn't do that.

He also could have taken James and John aside and struck a private bargain with them, saying something like, "Play it cool in front of the other guys, okay, boys? Keep up the good work and I'll see what strings I can pull for you with the Father." Jesus didn't do that either.

Jesus knew that this could easily become a no-win situation if he criticized or gave in to James and John. Either way, someone would be hurt and the team would be compromised. Yet he could not ignore the situation. Rather, he sidestepped the issue and put their request into a whole different context. How did he do it?

First of all, he stated that the reward the two disciples requested was not in his power to grant. Secondly, he redefined greatness, and therefore specialness of position, in terms of service. Jesus' ultimate message in this situation is "Do your job with dedication, to the best of your ability. Make a sincere and worthwhile contribution, not just to your organization but to your teammates as well, and have faith that your reward will come."

Jesus recognized their vain ambition, and he knew its divisive effect on his team. Yet he acted with love and forbearance. Without criticizing, he spelled out again for his disciples what really counts—loving service. He brought them back to their ultimate mission.

Notice his words. He didn't tell the disciples to *act like* a servant, but rather to *be* a servant. *Being* is a matter of one's essence. It's what you *are*. It's more encompassing than acting out a role. Jesus was telling them not just to demonstrate the *actions* of a servant, but also the *attitude* of a servant. The giving, in other words, must come not only from the hands, but also from the heart.

Jesus wanted his disciples to have, deep within, the *spirit* of service.

Whenever you have someone who frequently outperforms his or her teammates, you have a bird that bears watching. If this begins to interfere with team harmony, or the person is self-aggrandizing, it must be handled. You cannot ignore it. A no-win situation is brewing, and you need to intervene before it boils over. If it reaches the boiling point, the eruption may cause irreparable harm.

Handle it lovingly, as Jesus did. Read between the lines. Understand, if you can, the private ego-needs of the persons involved, yet don't let the superstar manipulate you.

Ultimately, the attitude of the superstar must also change, not just the behavior. Jesus zeroed in on attitude as well as action when he dealt with his overly personally ambitious disciples. He carefully spelled out the parameters of how greatness was to come in his organization, and how his people would be evaluated. You need to do the same.

Jesus did another curious thing. He didn't give in to James and John's request, but he didn't deny it, either! He said, "It is for those for whom it has been prepared." Who's to say that the honor couldn't go to James or John? Jesus wasn't baiting them. He was stating a fact. His implication—"Focus on your mission and your tasks. Have faith that the reward will come in its own time." This needs to be emphasized with your superstars as well.

When the superstars are into their egos, they're off track in terms of the organization as a whole. They need to be brought back to the central team goal in a way that makes emotional as well as logical sense to them. You need to approach them in a way that encourages them to *want* to play ball with the rest of their teammates. They obviously have high ego and recognition needs as well as achievement needs. They need help to channel their efforts in the right direction for the overall good.

Let's look at the team dynamics for a minute. What is it about superstars that turns their teammates off? Is it their consistent peak performance itself? A small percentage of teammates will be jealous of that, of course. But the real killers of team spirit are (1) a superior attitude on the part of the superstar and (2) disproportionately high recognition and favoritism by the leaders and observers!

In short, the onus is on you. The other players all benefit if the hero wins the game for them. Problems occur when the hero's status goes to his or her head.

Therefore, as the leader, help the superstar to develop the servant attitude that Jesus emphasized. Help him to see that his greatness will be enhanced if his teammates support him rather than envy him. Assist him to discover that the music of praise sounds much sweeter when it is played through the horns of others rather than through his own. Help him to be diligent in caring for his teammates rather than lording it over them.

And then, as the leader, practice the principle of individuality spelled out in Chapter 9. If you fail to recognize super achievement, their performance will wither like a plant without water. Put all the teammates' performance into perspective and find unique ways to recognize them all, both collectively and individually. If you make everyone feel legitimately important, the other players are much less liable to feel diminished by the stellar success of the superstar. Recognize his achievement, but don't treat him like a superstar. *Everyone's* input and output are critical to the overall success of the mission, and—in the final analysis—isn't that what really counts?

Look at what St. Paul wrote:

> For by the grace given to me I bid every one among you not to think of himself more highly than he ought to think, but to think with sober judgment, each according to the measure of faith which God has assigned him. For as in one body we have many members, and all the members do not have the same function, so we, though many, are one body in Christ, and individually members one of another. Having gifts that differ according to the grace given to us, let us use them: if prophecy, in proportion to our faith: if service, in our serving; he who teaches, in his teaching; he who exhorts, in his exhortation; he who contributes, in liberality; he who gives aid, with zeal; he who does acts of mercy, with cheerfulness.
>
> Rom. 12:3–8

One body, different parts, each carrying out a vital task. What better analogy is there for a well-functioning team?

22
HOW TO ATTACK

"Beware of practicing your piety before men in order to be seen by them; for then you will have no reward from your Father who is in heaven. Thus, when you give alms, sound no trumpet before you, as the hypocrites do in the synagogues and in the streets that they may be praised by men. Truly, I say to you, they have their reward. . . . And when you pray, you must not be like the hypocrites; for they love to stand and pray in the synagogues and at the street corners, that they may be seen by men. Truly, I say to you, they have their reward. . . . And when you fast, do not look dismal, like the hypocrites, for they disfigure their faces that their fasting may be seen by men. Truly, I say to you, they have their reward."

Matt. 6:1, 2, 5, 16

(*Parallel texts*: Mark 2:15–17; Luke 5:29–32)

While he was speaking, a Pharisee asked him to dine with him; so he went in and sat at table. The Pharisee was astonished to see that he did not first wash before dinner.

And the Lord said to him, "Now you Pharisees cleanse the outside of the cup and of the dish, but inside you are full of extortion and wickedness. You fools! Did not he who made the outside make the inside also? But give for alms those things which are within; and behold, everything is clean for you. But woe to the Pharisees! For you tithe mint and rue and every herb, and neglect justice and the love of God; these you ought to have done, without neglecting the others." ... One of the lawyers answered him, "Teacher, in saying this you reproach us also." And he said, "Woe to you lawyers also! for you load men with burdens hard to bear, and yourselves do not touch the burdens with one of your fingers. Woe to you! for you build the tombs of the prophets whom your fathers killed."

Luke 11:37–42, 45, 46

(*Parallel texts*: Matt. 23:25, 26)

Then said Jesus to the crowds and to his disciples, "The scribes and the Pharisees sit on Moses' seat; so practice and observe whatever they tell you, but not what they do; for they preach, but do not practice."

Matt. 23:1–3

For many who see Jesus as the loving leader, the compassionate Son of God, Jesus' scathing comments toward the Pharisees and scribes seem so uncharacteristic. Not at all.

To understand Jesus' words from a tactical point of view, we must explore who, why, and how he attacked. He did it in a very special way which is consistent throughout the preceding passages and in numerous other Gospel texts in which Jesus and the scribes and Pharisees confronted each other.

The Pharisees were a sect of Jewish religious adherents dedicated to the continuation of the law of Moses and its application to every aspect of daily life. These men were extremely concerned with maintaining the law and rabbinical tradition, and with keeping Judaism pure. In fact, the name *pharisee* means "separated one." The sect arose a couple of hundred years prior to Christ in reaction to the attempts of Antiochus Epiphanes of Syria to wipe out all evidence of Judaism and to replace it with Greek religion. We can imagine that the Pharisees of Jesus' day were just as concerned about maintaining the integrity of their religion since Israel was under Roman domination.

The Jewish law began with the Ten Commandments, followed by 613 mitzvoth or laws listed in the first five books of the Bible, which comprise the Torah. Since the time of Moses, thousands of minor laws and traditions governing every aspect of daily life were developed which became a part of the Jewish religion. The Pharisees were slavishly dedicated in practicing every one of these in their daily lives to demonstrate to God and men their religious purity and holiness. While they preached that others should do likewise, many Pharisees themselves practiced the law outwardly while inwardly they were on a religious ego trip, separating themselves from the common folk and showing little concern for their fellow men. It is this hypocrisy that Jesus was attacking, and this is what he meant in his reference to burdens in Luke 11:46.

The Pharisees were a necessary and vital part of Judaism. They preserved much of what is good and beautiful in Jewish tradition, and saved it from pagan obliteration. While many Pharisees at the time of Jesus were legitimately holy and devout servants of God, many more apparently had lost touch, if they ever had been in touch, with the humanistic intent of the law They were so intent on outward practice, obeying the letter of the law, that the spirit of the law was forgotten.

The Pharisees were zealous guardians of tradition. It is only natural that when Jesus, who was also a religious teacher with an increasing following, violated some of the traditions, they became insensed. Some of them challenged Jesus at every turn, seeing him as a threat, whereas other Pharisees could see Jesus' true intent and actually numbered themselves among his supporters.

Jesus, therefore, was not knocking all Pharisees and scribes, but was attacking the hypocrisy that many of them demonstrated. This is a vital distinction. Jesus never attacked specific persons, but rather he zeroed in on behavior.

Jesus' message was repentance and fitting oneself appropriately for the Kingdom of God. He exhorted people to be true to the spirit of the law, to show love, mercy, and service to one's neighbors. He preached putting things into perspective, not putting religious practices ahead of loving and serving God and humankind.

The hypocrisy practiced by the religious leaders, with their apparent hollowness of heart, stood in sharp contrast to Jesus' message. Naturally he attacked it, and very quickly engendered the wrath of those who felt his pressure.

How Jesus attacked is critical. His method always was "If the shoe fits . . ." Even in a direct confrontation with specific religious leaders, he never accused them by name. Rather he spoke of the class or group as a whole. Also he did not attack outright everything the Pharisees and scribes did, but only the hypocritical aspects of their behavior. Nowhere did he say that the scribes and Pharisees were evil men, but rather that many of the group did evil things. It was always left to the individual scribe or Pharisee to *determine for himself* whether or not he was guilty of what Jesus was condemning. Those who retaliated so vehemently saw that Jesus had clearly pegged *them*. They were also concerned that Jesus would topple everything they stood for, and diminish their fragile political acceptance by Rome.

Why did Jesus attack? First of all, their behavior stood in very sharp opposition to his message. In clear conscience he could not have done otherwise. The religious leaders had powerful sway over the people. The people were expected to follow their teachings to the letter. The religious leaders were asked to solve all kinds of legal and personal matters, and were thereby a vital force in everyday life. Religion, law, and politics were totally intertwined, and many religious leaders held national or local legal and political power as well, but of course, under the watchful eye of Rome. The scribes and Pharisees could not be ignored. The people had to be set straight because the essence of Judaism was being perverted by overlegalism and hypocrisy. Jesus knew that his mission centered around bringing people back to a right understanding of God. A spiritual "revolution" was necessary. There was no way Jesus could be quiet on these issues.

From a power perspective, however, there was another reason for his attack. A movement is not only defined by what it stands *for*. It often becomes more clearly defined by what it is *against*. Jesus needed opposition. By focusing on the religious hypocrisy of the leaders, he was able to create contrasts that made his own message clearer.

Creating a stand that brings out the opposition also creates emotion. Only when there is opposition are people put into a position of having to choose. By challenging the religious establishment, Jesus put the populace in the middle. The issues and choices became clear. Through his attack Jesus created a foil that added the power of popular emotion to his cause and created in his followers a feeling of missionary zeal. The power of conflict is that it keeps the zeal alive. When conflict ceases, people often lapse into complacency.

It's important to note that Jesus did not create the opposition to the hypocrisy of the religious establishment, nor did he challenge them simply to create an emotional ground swell. The Talmud itself spoke of hypocritical Pharisees. This issue was nothing new. The populace saw the Pharisees acting so piously every day of their lives, and undoubtedly quietly resented them for their outward show and misuse of power. So when Jesus condemned the leaders' behavior, the people, seeing Jesus as the spokesman for their own private feelings, probably shouted, "Right on!" Jesus wasn't, therefore, creating a straw man, but was highlighting a vital social issue.

Jesus' attacks had another important characteristic. He came out on the side of morals, purity, motherhood, and apple pie. To argue with him on these points was to condemn oneself.

Jesus' position was unassailable, invulnerable to a frontal attack. That's why his opponents had to create devious means to eliminate him.

There comes a time, if you're doing anything at all worthwhile, that you will face opposition and must take a stand. What can we learn from Jesus' methods that can enhance our power and effectiveness when that time arrives?

- Attack only for just cause. Never create phony opposition just to enhance your own power or to stir up your followers. Such a move will ultimately backfire, and you will be seen as a schemer and manipulator.
- Never attack specific individuals if you can help it. You want to avoid being seen as acting out a personal grudge.
- Attack the behavior, actions, or position a group may take, never the persons or group as a whole. As Jesus did, let your opponents condemn themselves through their actions. Use the "if the shoe fits" approach that Jesus demonstrated. That way you leave open the possibility of those from the opposing camp joining you if they, too, disagree with their own group on the issues you raise. By attacking the behavior or stance the opponents have taken, you inherently preserve their worth as persons. If they're "guilty" of what you claim, you can bet your booties that they will take it personally. But that's their decision. You will have kept your actions clean.
- Come out on the side of goodness, of principle. If you can back your attack with basic principles with which most people would agree, or with the good, benefit, or safety of your organization, you make a direct frontal attack very difficult. After all, right is on your side.
- Avoid prejudice. Praise your opposition for the good they have done. Act lovingly to individuals of the opposing party, and above all, treat them with respect (see Chapter 24).
- Maintain your honor. If they act dishonorably toward you, they only end up condemning themselves in the eyes of onlookers. Refuse to stoop to their level of unethical or dishon-

orable behavior. In a dirty fight, you cannot afford to compromise or sully your own hands, no matter how tempting it would be to return fire below the belt.

• Expect opposition and prepare for it. Study the issues, learn who your opponents will be. Be prepared for the worst, and hope it will never come. Carefully retain and practice the principles in the next three chapters. Jesus told his followers, "I send you out as sheep in the midst of wolves; so be as wise as serpents and innocent as doves" (Matt. 10:16).

Be wise as serpents and innocent as doves. When the time comes to take a stand, that is the only way to act. That's the only way to be assured that when the opposition hurls its mud at you, you can dodge most of it, and none of it will stick.

23
THE BEST DEFENSE

Jesus Before the Sanhedrin

The high priest (Annas) then questioned Jesus about his disciples and his teaching. Jesus answered him, "I have spoken openly to the world: I have always taught in synagogues and in the temple, where all Jews come together; I have said nothing secretly. Why do you ask me? Ask those who have heard me, what I said to them; they know what I said." When he had said this, one of the officers standing by struck Jesus with his hand, saying, "Is that how you answer the high priest?" Jesus answered him, "If I have spoken wrongly, bear witness to the wrong; but if I have spoken rightly, why do you strike me?" Annas then sent him bound to Caiaphas the high priest.

John 18:19–24

And some stood up and bore false witness against him, saying, "We heard him say, 'I will destroy this temple that is made with hands, and in three days I will build another, not made with hands.' '' Yet not even so did their testimony agree. And the high priest stood up in the midst, and asked Jesus, "Have you no answer to make? What is it that these men testify against you?" But he was silent and made no answer.

Mark 14:57–61a

And they said, "If you are the Christ, tell us." But he said to them, "If I tell you, you will not believe; and if I ask you, you will not answer. But from now on the Son of man shall be seated at the right hand of the power of God." And they all said, "Are you the Son of God, then?" And he said to them, "You say that I am." And they said, "What further testimony do we need? We have heard it ourselves from his own lips."

Luke 22:66b–71

(*Parallel texts:* Matt. 26:59–66; Mark 14:61b–64)

Jesus Before Pontius Pilate, the Roman Governor

Now Jesus stood before the governor; and the governor asked him, "Are you the King of the Jews?" Jesus said to him, "You have said so." But when he was accused by the chief priests and elders, he made no answer. Then Pilate said to him, "Do you not hear how many things they testify against you?" But he gave him no answer, not even to a single charge; so that the governor wondered greatly.

Matt. 27:11–14

Pilate entered the praetorium again and called Jesus, and said to him, "Are you the King of the Jews?" Jesus answered, "Do you say this of your own accord, or did others say it to you about me?" Pilate answered, "Am I a Jew? Your own nation and the chief priests have handed you over to me; what have you done?" Jesus answered, "My kingship is not of this world; if my kingship were of this world, my servants would fight, that I might not be handed

over to the Jews; but my kingship is not from the world."
Pilate said to him, "So you are a king?" Jesus answered,
"You say that I am a king. For this I was born, and for this
I have come into the world, to bear witness to the truth.
Every one who is of the truth hears my voice."

John 18:33–37

(*Parallel texts: Mark 15:2–5; Luke 23:2–5*)

Jesus Before Herod

And when [Pilate] learned that he belonged to Herod's
jurisdiction, he sent him over to Herod, who was himself
in Jerusalem at that time. When Herod saw Jesus, he was
very glad, for he had long desired to see him, because he
had heard about him, and he was hoping to see some
sign done by him. So he questioned him at some length;
but he made no answer.

Luke 23:7–9

In your defenselessness lies your power.

Jesus faced a kangaroo court if ever there was one. He was
condemned before his trial began, and he knew it. Let's take a
moment and consider what was going on.

Jesus was first taken to Annas, the former high priest (from
A.D. 6 to 15) and father-in-law to Caiaphas, who was high priest
at that time. No doubt Annas had it in for Jesus. Annas and his
family, through currying favor and collaborating with Rome,
had, in essence, bought the high priesthood. After Annas held
the high priest's office, four of his sons held it, and now Caiaphas was in office. Annas's family was extremely wealthy
through ill-gotten gain. His family controlled the Temple treasury and the selling of sacrifices within the Temple precinct,
charging exorbitant prices for blemishless sacrificial animals.
They gouged the public, and it was these "money changers"
whom Jesus overthrew a few days before his trial.[1] The common folk hated Annas and his family, and so Jesus' action
could have sparked a rebellion. Jesus attacked Annas in his

pocketbook, and we can just imagine the glee that Annas must have felt having Jesus in his clutches.

Innocent enough to us as twentieth-century readers, Jesus' "trial" before Annas was actually a travesty of justice. Traditional Jewish legal practice forbade the questioning of the accused in any manner that could incriminate him. As Maimonides, the medieval Jewish scholar, wrote, "Our true law does not inflict the penalty of death upon a sinner by his own confession."[2] Thus, when John states, "The High Priest questioned Jesus . . ." this approach was totally out of line, legally irregular. Jesus knew this. That's why he responded, "Why do you ask me questions? Ask those who heard me. . . ." Jesus knew that according to Jewish law, incriminating evidence could be accepted only from others, from witnesses, never from the accused himself. In this statement, Jesus held his ground, refusing to give in, asking for proper justice.

Then Jesus was hauled before Caiaphas and the Sanhedrin, the religious supreme court. The chief priests, scribes, and elders of the people had been assembled in the wee hours of the morning. False witnesses were summoned to testify against Jesus, again because according to Jewish law, incriminating evidence can come only from others. Of course, the court botched it. The testimony of their hurriedly called "witnesses" did not agree. So again, contrary to accepted legal practice, Jesus was asked to incriminate himself.

Notice the control and dignity Jesus must have maintained before the court in spite of his undoubtedly bruised and disheveled personal appearance. He refused to respond to the allegations, and when asked about whether he was the Messiah, he responded with a tremendously powerful statement. Let's look at it carefully to see why the Sanhedrin were so disturbed.

Jesus had continually referred to himself, at least throughout the latter part of his ministry, as "the Son of Man," a term probably equivalent to Messiah but implying divinity and supernatural power. Here, in response to Caiaphas, he identified himself with God by stating that "the Son of man shall be seated at the right hand of the power of God." No wonder the council was threatened.

But Jesus carried his claim further. The accounts of Matthew and Luke state that Jesus responded to the direct question with "You say that I am." However, Mark, the earliest Gospel, shows Jesus as responding, "I am."

To Caiaphas and the council, these words were blasphemy. When Moses was first encountered by God in the wilderness, he asked God what His name was. God replied, "I Am Who I Am," and He said, "Say this to the people of Israel, 'I Am has sent me to you' " (Ex. 3:14). I Am was the earliest and most sacred title for God, and was so holy that it was never to be uttered by mankind. In his response, Jesus not only uttered the unutterable, thus violating sacred tradition, he applied the holiest name of God to himself. Now we can see why Caiaphas, according to Matthew's account, was so vehement that he tore his robes.

Pilate approached Jesus' situation from a different point of view. Pilate didn't care about the religious issues involved, but judged him from the civil perspective, and, of course, found no civil crimes. Yet he was swayed by the pressure from the religious authorities. Again, Jesus took the same tack. He made no defense against the charges. When Jesus was sent to Herod, he responded in the same way to Herod's questions.

Why didn't Jesus defend himself?

First of all, he knew that whatever he said would fall on deaf ears. Why try to convince a prejudiced person? Jesus knew that reason and logic alone would be to no avail. This was a setup; death was a foregone conclusion. When emotions are involved, when the accusers have an ax to grind and are not open-minded, no amount of truth will sway them as long as they are wedded to their falsehoods. From a tactical point of view, never argue with an emotional person, never try to "logic" a prejudiced individual. It won't work. You will do yourself more harm than good to try to talk yourself out of a situation when the cards are stacked against you.

Secondly, power was at stake. In Chapter 2 we discussed the power advantage of a questioner over the one who is being questioned. If Jesus had attempted to defend himself against the false witnesses, or explain himself to the Sanhedrin, they would have had Jesus on the run, they would have been one up. They would have won the power contest, because they would have succeeded in putting Jesus on the defensive.

But Jesus didn't fall for that game. He stated his case in one sentence and made no further testimony. This is a deeper reason for the council's ire—Jesus frustrated their power play by his silence. He didn't lose the power contest in court because he didn't play!

Thirdly, he forced the Sanhedrin to break their own laws in order to condemn him. He refused to incriminate himself, and since there were no valid witnesses, there was no reason for the death penalty other than the Sanhedrin's fear of popular revolt and the possible loss of their personal power should Rome see that they could not manage their people. By his silence, Jesus gave them nothing legitimate with which to crucify him. Thus the court had to act unjustly if it wanted Jesus eliminated.

Fourthly, Jesus maintained his dignity through not stooping so low as to rebut ridiculous, fallacious accusations. Some verbal assaults are so ludicrous that they are not worth rebutting. If you do answer such claims, the fact that you pay attention to them may cause observers to wonder if there is any truth in them. The false witnesses hung themselves, for their testimony did not agree. Why should Jesus bother to respond?

There may be times when we are put "on trial." We may be called upon to back up our claims, to defend a position to a hostile audience, to argue a point that disagrees with prevailing opinion, or even to answer charges brought by others who would see us disgraced or unseated from a position of power. What tactical lessons is Jesus teaching us from his behavior at his trial?

Lesson Number One—first and foremost—is that in your defenselessness lies your power. It takes courage to be defenseless. By "defenseless" I mean not going on the defensive, not making excuses, not throwing up verbal shields to protect yourself. Most people, when confronted, try to weasel out or explain their actions away. They start running scared, they're sweating hard. In their fear, they often stumble over their words, make conflicting statements, and dig their hole even deeper. Thus they become their own worst enemy.

Jesus was "defenseless." He was cool and calm. He stated his claim in one or two sentences, and remained silent. He retained, and actually enhanced, his dignity by refusing to respond to lies and inappropriate questioning. His silence made Pilate wonder, and infuriated his accusers. That was actually a sign that Jesus was winning. In a power contest, the loser often becomes angry as he or she realizes that the goal of putting the accused on his guard has failed.

Another way to phrase Lesson Number One is "Maintain your dignity." Often the best way to do this is to follow Jesus' example. State your case simply and powerfully, and then be quiet. By so doing, you maintain your power and self-control, even if you're being grilled alive. No one can make you answer when you don't wish to respond. Never forget that, even in an inquisition, you are still in control of you, and no one can take that control away.

Lesson Number Two—Never cast your pearls before swine. In other words, read the climate. Are the people who are challenging you open-minded? Can they be swayed by logic? Or are they prejudiced, blind to reason, unwilling to change their minds? When the latter is the case, as it was with Jesus, never try to reason with them. Reason means nothing to prejudiced people, or to hostile ones. Their minds are made up; don't confuse them with facts. They will only twist what you say and use it against you. Now, in power terms, this is precisely what prejudiced accusers want to do. They defeat you by twisting your words. In the ensuing power contest, they win, you lose.

The winner is the one with the last word, and you can be certain that when your accusers come back at you with twisted logic, the last word won't be yours.

Lesson Number Three—refuse to fear the consequences. Here's where faith under fire comes in. This is the basic spiritual principle—God will take care of you. He will give you the words to say, and will turn the outcome into opportunity and a blessing. Trust the principle. Take heart, and leave your fate to the Lord. He *will* provide.

Jesus knew this. His trial was the beginning of the culmination of his mission on earth. He could endure the pain and face the end unafraid, for he knew that he was already in God's hands. How then could men prevail against him?

One way to beat fear is to ask yourself what the worst thing is that could happen. If you identify the worst-case scenario, and then look at the possible options, you may find ways to squeeze victory out of defeat, to turn adversity into opportunity.

Another way is to pray. Ask for courage and guidance, and then visualize yourself handling the situation with calm, courage, and dignity. All the suggestions in Chapter 11 apply here.

This chapter focused on tactics for a specific situation. There is an underlying principle and an attitude that enhances the power of these tactics. To discover what that principle is, read the next chapter.

24
HANDLING THE OPPOSITION

"But I say to you that hear, Love your enemies, do good to those who hate you, bless those who curse you, pray for those who abuse you."

Luke 6:27–28

(*Parallel text*: Matt. 5:43)

"But I say to you, Do not resist one who is evil. But if any one strikes you on the right cheek, turn to him the other also; and if any one would sue you and take your coat, let him have your cloak as well."

Matt. 5:39–40

(*Parallel text*: Luke 6:39)

This is one of the most difficult sayings of Jesus. It certainly flies in the face of our modern conventional "fight fire with fire" wisdom. Yet turning the other cheek is precisely what Jesus did at his trial. In a world in which might still makes right, a "passive" response to opposition appears to be folly.

If someone accosts you with a gun, will you hand him a rose? We know that maintaining a balance of power internationally requires a strong military preparedness in order to preserve peace. Is Jesus saying that we should submit to tyranny? Probably not. But when it comes to much of the opposition that we may face on a daily basis, turning the other cheek proves to be the folly of a fox.

Jesus' metaphor reaches far beyond slaps on the face. In today's parlance, Jesus might be saying, "Rise above insults. Show grace under fire."

As a leader, you are more visible by definition. And because you are more visible, you become a larger target. Opposition can come in at least two forms. First there will almost always be some who resent you for your position or your actions. They may harbor quiet resentment, complain about you behind your back, or even secretly or openly attempt to sabotage you. Not uncommonly, they will criticize you "on principle," but their thinly veiled competitiveness or jealousy quickly becomes apparent to the perceptive observer. Jealous opposition often stems from feelings of being hurt, threatened, ignored, or passed over. Second, there may be those who oppose you honestly. They disagree with you, but wish you no ill. They just have a different point of view. With these folks, debating the issues may be useful. You may be able to win them over, or they may show you points that you have not considered.

With jealous opponents, debate is rarely practical, because the attack is really being carried out at the personal level. These people need to beat you, make you defensive, put you on the run. Once you start defending yourself to these people, you are lost.

Some attacks are so ridiculous that they are not worth rebutting. In fact, in that case, to waste your time even casually denying them may make your listeners wonder if there is actually some truth to them. Other opposition is so potentially damaging that it begs rebuttal. In fact, you might even lose sleep over the temptation to attack in kind.

Let's look at what's going on when you face jealous opposition. The issue here is power—who gains the upper hand. The game is played at the emotional level. The outward variations are endless, but the underlying interpersonal dynamics are almost always the same. Regardless of the outcome on the surface, at the emotional level, the opponents win in the beginning, at the instant that they can get you hooked emotionally. They win at the point that you become defensive and feel the need to retaliate. Hooking you and getting you on the defensive is the goal. If that is achieved, they have secured the victory. The rest, even the final outcome, is the cost of war, a price that is often willingly paid. This same mechanism explains why a child will defy a parent, risk punishment and even physical abuse.

There is tremendous power in being able to manipulate others from a state of calm to one of rage or defensiveness. Power is a vertical issue: who is above and who is below. If you are the leader, you are above. If I am jealous or feel a need to defeat you, I am placing myself one down or below you, I perceive my self-esteem to be threatened, and therefore, I must turn the tables. I may not be able to get you knocked out of your actual leadership position, but I can get emotional power over you if I can get you on the defensive. Metaphorically, I then become the judge and you become the defendant. If I can achieve this, then, I'm on top psychologically—I win and you lose.

A friend of mine supervises several workers older than she. The older workers resent this young whippersnapper's telling them what to do. They treat her coldly and are often critical. She is annoyed and hurt, and has been tempted to retaliate. The older workers got under her skin. She thought about them day and night. Her job was becoming increasingly miserable, and in spite of her obvious capability, she began to think about changing jobs. What could she do?

Jesus is saying that the solution to this competitive power game is not to play. His answer is to rise above insult and to return evil with good. Is this practical?

You have your public image to consider. No matter how private the motive of your opponents, they will usually make some of their moves public, because they will want to gain supporters. If they sling mud in your direction, you will be seen by others as reducing yourself to their level if your sling it back. While it excites us to see it fly, most of us inwardly detest mudslinging, and those who do it ultimately destroy their credibility.

Then there is the issue of "style." President Carter attacked Reagan in the presidential debate in the 1980 campaign. At the end of the debate, Reagan immediately left his lectern, strode over to Carter, and shook his hand. In that move, Reagan clearly outstyled Carter. We admire courage and grace under fire. If you keep your cool and act graciously, you will gain more support. By "killing them with kindness," you take a giant step toward neutralizing your opposition. They will begin to look ridiculous if they keep attacking a person who is "too big to fight back." Perhaps you will even win them over.

But Jesus was talking about more than strategy. He was referring to a basic attitude. An attitude of love that stretches beyond family, friends, and supporters to include our opponents. Again, the folly of a fox! If you *really* want to *understand* your opponents, you need to develop a true, positive appreciation for them. That's the only way you can fully empathize with them, feel their pulse beat. If you are hung up on anger or righteous indignation, your vision is blocked and skewed by your feelings and biases. Anger blocks out understanding. And you can't adequately cope with or manage someone whom you don't understand or respect.

Furthermore, while anger increases motivation, it reduces precision. Angry people make more mistakes. If your opponents get you all worked up, you may slip up, and they will have an additional tactical advantage. One big mistake you might make would be to take your mind and energy off your own strategy and the task at hand, and invest it in a futile attempt to get even. Cool's the rule, hot gets shot!

Jesus said, "Pray for those who abuse you." Think about the

implications of this if you were to do it earnestly, honestly, and lovingly. Would you dare to do this? Where would your anger go? Love takes courage, but it also brings courage. Love and fear cannot coexist; love requires letting go of fear. Only when fear and worry are significantly reduced is love possible. By learning to love your opponents, you are taking the most courageous and noble stance possible.

How to react to your opponents?

- Consider them a compliment. Often the merit of an idea or action can be measured by the opposition it receives. Incurring opposition may mean that you're doing something significant.
- Consider them an opportunity. By having to answer or cope with opponents, you solidify, and often clarify, your own position. Opponents make you think sharply and won't let you become lazy.
- Consider them a resource. Sometimes it pays to attempt to win them over, especially if they are of the "honest" variety, wishing you no personal ill.
- Let go of anger and fear, rise above hostility. Grace under fire is associated with maturity, while becoming petulant and losing your cool is considered immature.
- Try to understand and empathize with them. Look for the basic feelings and attitudes that sparked their opposition in the first place. If you uncover these, you may be able to do something that helps them reduce these feelings.
- Treat them kindly, graciously, and with respect. Show that you appreciate and admire their positive contributions. Don't discourage, but give them every consideration that you would give to your loyal friends. A friend of mine once said, "Where you don't find love, put it. Then you will find it."
- Pray for them. It's so tempting to ask God to punish them or help them see the error of their ways (which so often translates to, "God, help them to agree with me"). Rather, ask God to bless them, heal their hurt, or whatever their positive need

might be. This will help heal not only them, but you as well. You can't remain angry very long toward those whom, through prayer, you bring to the Throne of Grace.

My friend who supervises the older workers was advised to consider the source. Before second-guessing herself, she needed to understand where her opponents were coming from emotionally and to figure out their strategy. She decided to treat them with obvious, but not overdone, friendliness. She greeted them every day and responded in a cheerful way to them whenever she had contact with them. At first, she couldn't see herself pulling this off, but when she thought of it as a "retraining" period and a tactical maneuver, she felt more comfortable with her plan. Gradually her opponents were worn down. It became increasingly difficult to fight her in the face of her friendliness. While she and the older supervisees never became real friends, day by day management became easier, cooperation in the unit improved, and most of all, my friend felt in control of the situation and her effectiveness as a leader was enhanced.

It doesn't always work out this way. In some situations disciplinary action may be required. Every situation is different and must be assessed on its own merits. But if you face opposition, the ball is in your court. You must cope in some way. Will you fall victim to their ploys or will you rise above?

The choice is yours. But let's never forget that by turning the other cheek, Gandhi drove the entire British Empire to its knees.

25
THE FINEST HOUR

> And when they came to the place which is called The Skull, there they crucified him, and the criminals, one on the right and one on the left. And Jesus said, "Father, forgive them; for they know not what they do."
>
> Luke 23:33, 34a

Jesus spoke these words from the cross. What a remarkable attitude: he was forgiving, and probably loving, those who drove in the nails, and those many who were implicated in some way in his crucifixion. Most likely he even included Judas, who had betrayed him. In any event, these words are far more than vainglory or a futile show of nobleness in the face of death, or a gallows-graciousness. Jesus had a deep sense of compassion that showed through, even at his own execution.

What was Jesus really doing? Was he making excuses for shoddy behavior? Was he saying, "God, please let these guys off the hook because they don't know it's a sin to kill someone"? No way! He was allowing for their humanness, their misunderstanding, their blind ignorance to his ultimate mission. He was asking forgiveness for his opponents who could not see who Jesus was because they were blinded by their own biases, their own misconceptions. Because of their blindness, they acted inappropriately, even to the point of committing the ultimate crime.

But is it a crime to execute a felon? The leaders who schemed Jesus' elimination were trying to protect themselves, their religious establishment, and perhaps their nation, from the power of Rome. Jesus' death was a political setup.

What was Jesus really asking God to forgive? The nail drivers? Yes. But also much more. His opponents' attitudes as well as their actions. Perhaps he was saying to God, "Take time to understand these people. They acted out of misconception, out of basic human motives. They're not 'murderers'; they're just mistaken." Implicit in his prayer is the request, "Back off, God. Think this through. Don't overreact out of haste or revenge. Sort out the context."

How often do we blow up and engage in a witch hunt when someone makes a crucial error? We can yell and scream, throw a tantrum, and fire the guy. But this is a luxury the true leader can ill afford. It's wise to recall that all too often the desire to punish carries with it feelings of jealousy, rage, and a desire to get even—emotions that are all too transparent to others in a punishment situation.

When someone else errs, show graciousness. Hold him or her accountable for the mistake or the misbehavior and act appropriately, but take into account the possibility of miscommunication, of mistaken understanding, and of human failing.

Look to salvage the situation and the person involved, if at all possible. Did he or she fail because of a lack of some information, resource, or skill? If so, isn't it better to find out and rectify it so the same mistake doesn't happen in the future?

The savvy leader knows that punishment without forgiveness is a jump-to-solution without a thorough understanding of the relevant problem or people. Apart from the human downside of punishment, there is perhaps a more fatal risk for the leader: the notion that once we've punished the perpetrator, the problem is solved. This is a double risk. First, if we punish as a knee-jerk reaction and fail to analyze, then we risk that the problem isn't really solved or even accurately diagnosed. Therefore, it can happen again. If this happens, and you're the responsible one, whose face will wear the egg? Second, the one you punish may well turn against you. He or she may go underground and whip up a ground swell of opposition, and will seize any opportunity to undermine you now or in the future.

In Chapter 24 I noted that, at the end of the Ronald Reagan/ Jimmy Carter presidential debate, Reagan left his lectern and walked over to shake Carter's hand. That, according to numerous analysts, won him the debate. In that one gracious gesture, Reagan outstyled Carter.

True graciousness is not just a matter of style. If your style is only skin-deep, it will quickly become apparent to those around you. Rather, grace must come from within, from a heartfelt attitude of human generosity and caring. Forgiveness is perhaps the ultimate test of grace.

True forgiveness sometimes requires high levels of emotional maturity. Ego must be put aside. We can't forgive if we're still licking our wounds. For then all we taste is bitterness.

Being nailed to a cross was the ultimate degradation. Yet this was not where Jesus was fixing his mind. He had to rise above natural human rage and see beyond the torture and pain of the moment.

A personal attack is perhaps the hardest thing to forgive. If it is severe enough, with important consequences, we may nurse hurt feelings and/or harbor rage for days, weeks, even years. This is our natural reaction, our first response. Unless we're in supercontrol, a hostile knee-jerk reaction is all but inevitable.

Yet in the face of a personal attack, the true leader needs to demonstrate the uncommon reaction—a cool head and graciousness, even forgiveness, in private as well as in public.

This goes without saying as you read these words, but it's so hard to accomplish when you're under the gun. Forgiveness takes the principles of the last chapter to the ultimate level.

What does it mean to forgive? Listen to what God is saying about Israel through the prophet Jeremiah:

> "And no longer shall each man teach his neighbor and each his brother, saying 'Know the Lord,' for they shall all know me, from the least of them to the greatest, says the Lord; for I will forgive their iniquity, and I will remember their sin no more."
>
> Jer. 31:34

Here is the ultimate statement about forgiveness—to *remember the sin no more*. Forgive *and* forget. How often we glibly roll that phrase off our tongues —"forgive and forget"— without really taking it seriously. How often do we say, "I can forgive, but I can't forget"?

To forgive without forgetting is a contradiction in terms, and therefore impossible. Does forgiveness mean erasing the offense from our memory entirely? Ultimately yes, but in our humanity, this is often not easily accomplished. Small offenses may be quickly forgotten when we choose to stop nursing our hurt, anger, and indignation and get on with life. Greater or major offenses are much more difficult to eradicate.

Many women say that although the pain of labor is excruciating, it is all forgotten in the joy of the actual moment of birth, and in seeing and holding the newborn child. So it should be with forgiveness. While we may have a recollection of the offending incident and its consequences, the emotional component has been worked through. The nerve center to our feelings of anger and retaliation has been shut down. Once forgiven, the recollection will no longer trigger a hostile reaction. And nothing will shut down this emotional hot wire faster than a deeply developed attitude of understanding and compassion. Forgiveness is the balm that heals broken relationships.

The way to prepare yourself is to develop your attitude of graciousness and compassion as strongly as you can every day. Let's never forget that most often, for practical purposes, the difference between a minor peccadillo and a major offense is how you choose to perceive the incident. Overlook what can reasonably be overlooked. Look behind the obvious. Don't jump to conclusions nor act upon your first reaction without thinking it through and putting yourself into the offender's shoes. If disciplinary action is required, it must be taken. Yet discipline, to be a positive growth experience for the offender, must be meted out without the emotions of anger, rage, or the desire to punish or get even.

Make graciousness a basic value, a daily habit. Only then can you pull it off for real when the chips are down. Only then can forgiveness become a natural response from the cross.

And what is a practical definition of forgiveness, anyway? The ability to go on together after the difficulty, with your relationship uninterrupted and unimpaired.

AFTERWORD
THE RELIGIOUS SCENE
IN JESUS' DAY

There were several important religious groups with whom Jesus interacted within the course of his life and ministry. Most of these have been mentioned in the text of this book, so we don't need to elaborate on them here.

The Zealots, as stated in Chapter 7, were a radical nationalistic group who acted for the overthrow of Rome and a return to the Law of Moses. They staged insurrections throughout Palestine and had a band of political hit men whose role was to assassinate their oppressors without regard to their own lives. Their revolts grew until they finally instigated the Jewish-Roman War (A.D. 66–70), at the end of which the Jewish state was subjugated and the Temple was again destroyed. Simon, one of Jesus' disciples, was a Zealot, but it is doubtful from Jesus' message that he supported this movement, even though he was probably considered a Zealot by Pilate.

The Pharisees and scribes were described in Chapter 22. Jesus attacked them for their hypocrisy, but also had several, perhaps many, adherents from within their ranks. While the

Pharisees and scribes were culturally and religiously very important, they did not hold tremendous political influence.

Political dominance probably was held by the Sadducees. They belonged to Jerusalem's priestly class, and they readily cooperated with Rome, which legitimized their power. Along with the Pharisees and elders of the people, they comprised the Sanhedrin. They were theologically conservative, and did not believe in the resurrection of the dead.

The scribes, since the time of Ezra, were doctors of the law. They were the main teachers in the synagogues and were highly respected. Their opinions were daily sought in both legal and religious matters. Scribes did not comprise a religious or political party in and of themselves. Anyone could be a scribe who underwent their rigorous educational preparation. They were accorded the places of honor in the synagogues and were commonly addressed as "rabbi."

Another group was the Essenes, made famous in recent years through the discovery of the Dead Sea Scrolls at Qumran. The Essenes lived a monastic life in the desert, choosing to separate themselves from the pressures and strains of life in the cities and towns. They rejected the priesthood in Jerusalem, and hoped to develop the "true Israel." They spent much of their time in the study of Scripture and adhered to strict religious traditions. Jesus appeared to have little contact with this group, although John the Baptist may have been an Essene. Some theorists have linked Jesus with the Essenes, but his ministry and message were completely uncharacteristic of this group.

An additional group of an entirely different nature were the natives of the region of Samaria, or the Samaritans. Samaria included the central area of Palestine, above Jerusalem and below Galilee. They were not a political group per se. Religiously, they claimed to descend from the Israelites of the Northern Kingdom (Israel, as opposed to the southern kingdom of Judah). The Samaritans worshiped the same God, but had intermarried down through the years with foreigners. They were hated by the Jews for many years before Jesus came onto the scene. They were not permitted to worship at the Temple in Jerusalem, and Jews were not permitted to have any dealings with Samaritans. The Samaritans responded in kind, and built their own temple on Mount Gerizim and had their own version of the Torah. Thus it is quite significant that the hero of one of Jesus' most famous parables was a Samaritan.

Much could be said about the life and times of the historical Jesus. Myriad volumes have been written about Jesus and his mission on earth. This brief Afterword has been supplied to highlight some of the context in which Jesus lived and preached. My aim throughout this book has been to shed light on a particular aspect of Jesus—his charismatic techniques in motivating and managing people. Jesus has been a model for many of us in our private lives. He is also a model for inspired management and motivation in our businesses and organizations as well.

It is one thing to have faith. It's quite another to put that faith into action. Often we are unsure of how to proceed, of what techniques to use.

If this small book has helped you with the vital issue of "how to" incorporate the techniques of Jesus into your leadership style, it has all been worthwhile to write and publish it. If this book has helped you to more fully appreciate and inject the *spirit* of Jesus into your leadership style, may God be praised.

If we wish to be transformational leaders, we must become *transformed* leaders, carrying deep within ourselves the spirit of love and power—the Spirit of God. As Jesus said:

> "Let your light so shine before men, that they may see your good works, and give glory to your Father who is in heaven."
>
> Matt. 5:16

Notes

For more information on the historical aspects of Jesus' life and ministry, consult the following:

Encyclopaedia Britannica, 15th ed., s.v. "Jesus Christ."
John Reumann, *Jesus of Nazareth: Son of God, Son of Man* (Philadelphia: Lutheran Church Press, 1966), 9–21.

REFERENCES

Chapter 1

1. H. A. Olson, *The New Way to Compete: How to Discover Your Personal Competitive Style and Make It Work for You* (Lexington, Mass.: D. C. Heath, Lexington Books, 1990), 162, 163.

2. Abraham Lincoln, "Gettysburg Address."

Chapter 2

1. Joan C. Harvey and Cynthia Katz, *If I'm So Successful, Why Do I Feel Like a Fake?* (New York: St. Martin's Press, 1985), 2, 3.

2. Gerald Ferris, cited in *Executive Fitness Newsletter* 20, no. 12 (December 1989).

3. "Quiet Moves That Convey Untold Clout," *Personal Report for the Executive* (December 1, 1989): 1, 2.

Chapter 3

For further information directly relevant to the recommendations in this chapter, you may wish to read H. A. Olson,

The New Way to Compete: How to Discover Your Personal Competitive Style and Make It Work for You (Lexington, Mass.: D. C. Heath, Lexington Books, 1990), Chaps. 7–9.

Chapter 4

1. M. Bragg and N. Jewison, *Jesus Christ Superstar*. Universal Pictures, 1973.

Chapter 7

1. William Barclay, *The Gospel of Matthew*, rev. ed., vol. 1 (Philadelphia: Westminster Press, 1975), 78–79.

Chapter 9

For further information on competition and comparison, review:

1. H. A. Olson, *The New Way to Compete* (Lexington, Mass.: D. C. Heath, Lexington Books, 1990), and A. Kohn, *No Contest: The Case Against Competition* (Boston: Houghton-Mifflin, 1986).

Chapter 10

1. William Barclay, *The Gospel of Matthew*, rev. ed., vol. 1 (Philadelphia: Westminster Press, 1975), 88, 89.

2. Ibid.

Chapter 23

1. William Barclay, *The Gospel of John*, rev. ed., vol. 2 (Philadelphia: Westminster Press, 1975), 225, 226.

2. Ibid., 227.